I was TRAPPED
in a Miserable Marriage and Screwed by the Terrible System!

Z Publishing

Disclaimer: Although this is a work of nonfiction, some names, places, dates, and time frames have been altered for artistic and continuity reasons, as well as for vetting and legal purposes.

The opinions expressed in this manuscript are solely the opinions of the author and do not represent the opinions or thoughts of the publisher. The author has represented and warranted full ownership and/or legal right to publish all the materials in this book.

I was TRAPPED in a Miserable Marriage and Screwed by the Terrible System!
All Rights Reserved.
Copyright © 2014 J. Golf
v2.0

Cover Photo © 2014 JupiterImages Corporation. All rights reserved - used with permission.

This book may not be reproduced, transmitted, or stored in whole or in part by any means, including graphic, electronic, or mechanical without the express written consent of the publisher except in the case of brief quotations embodied in critical articles and reviews.

ISBN: 978-0-578-13438-3

PRINTED IN THE UNITED STATES OF AMERICA

Contents

INTRODUCTION 1
THE STORY 5
THE FILING 29
HAZEL 51
HER DEPOSITION 53
MY DEPOSITION 59
MEDIATION 63
ADVICE SECTION 78

INTRODUCTION

I started saving money from mowing yards and babysitting when I was fourteen years old. When I was fifteen, I became a busboy at a country club and then a waiter at sixteen. I was always steadfast in throwing money into savings out of each paycheck. I got a job as a jailer at eighteen for the local county sheriff's department and then as a meter reader (big pay raise) a year later. I worked seven years at the electric company, moving into accounting and then customer service before leaving to work in the career that I still do today as a salesman for an aluminum mill (more than twenty-five years). I tell you all of this so you will later understand how painful it is to give more than half of your money away through a divorce to someone who has never believed in saving one freaking dime! More than thirty-five years of hard-earned savings, GONE, worse than the 2008 stock market correction that also cost me close to half of my net worth. It reminds me of the joke where the guy is telling his buddies that he lost half of his net worth in the stock market crash, but he still had his wife. My money went to a working wife of nineteen years, not a stay-at-home homemaker. She earned between $60,000 and $80,000 per year cleaning teeth. I think she is better at cleaning out husbands than she is cleaning teeth! With all those years of income, guess how much she actually put in the bank. ZERO.

Anyway, I tell you all of this to set the stage for the true story I am going to reveal about my life and marriage to B. I am going to refer to her as B, because if I used her real name, I would probably get sued. She is famous for filing lawsuits and is addicted to lawyers and the power she feels when she has them on the payroll. Oh yeah, these are lawyers that she does not actually pay. She finds lawyers that will take contingency arrangements or ones that come after me for their attorney fees, because she does not have a dime in the bank. I am sure there may be other stories out there that may compare to mine or possibly be worse; however, I have a whole heck of a lot of friends and customers, and no one can believe what I put up with or how this entire process went for me.

Years ago, one of my best friends went through a divorce, and he spent almost $50,000 in attorney fees. I wanted to throw up for him! I could not believe that any idiot would spend $50,000 in attorney fees just

INTRODUCTION

to get a divorce. I know many friends that have gone through it for under $3,000. WELL, MY FRIENDS, I am going to make all of those divorced folks out there feel a little bit better about their attorney bill once you hear of my grand total. I will explain what I mean by being trapped in a marriage with no way out. I will also spend some time on advice that I believe I am worthy of lending, since being dragged through the miserable process. It is a process that you don't really have a choice in, but there are sure some better ways to tackle it, and I wish someone had given me the advice I am going to share. I am not a certified or trained expert in the field, but certainly have some firsthand on-the-job training of what I experienced and what I would do differently. I feel like I have a Ph.D. in "getting screwed!"

Even after the twenty-year marriage, the first ten years were OK, I am not bitter toward women or marriage. I believe I will be married again, as I can't be so unlucky to land another B. I want someone to grow old with and to sit on the front porch swing and hold hands with when I am seventy-five. Years ago, I knew that person was not B, but I stayed in there for many reasons that you will learn about in my story, and it sure cost me in the end. I do believe that I was married to a one-in-a-million person. Don't you almost feel like it would be impossible to lose twenty straight hands of blackjack at the casino? Well, that too has

◀ I WAS TRAPPED IN A MISERABLE MARRIAGE AND SCREWED BY THE TERRIBLE SYSTEM!

happened in my life. I really just don't believe this could happen to me again. Just like all those people who play the lottery, the odds are better of dying in a plane crash. So if you win the lottery, should you avoid all airplane flights for the rest of your life? I am not going to let B ruin the opportunity I may have to share a loving relationship with someone I really want to care for and take care of, during sickness or health and for better or worse. My worse with B just kept getting more worse, and the sickness was the fact that she is probably bipolar or has some mental disorder that she refused to acknowledge or have analyzed. She thinks everyone else is the whack- job in her fuzzy little simple mind. Probably the reason she has had more than forty jobs since I have known her is that she cannot get along with others, especially women. It is always THEIR fault when she would tell me of her quitting her job AGAIN. Well, I hate to make this an entire bash session of B, even though this is MY book, and I can use this as a mode to vent, if I want to. I will get on with my story, and please trust me that everything I am about to tell you is true. If you are in a situation like this, PRAY HARD.

THE STORY BACKGROUND

I was born in Kentucky in 1962 to two wonderful people. They were great parents. My dad was a little on the strict side (ex-marine) and he had some quirks, but it was never doubted that he loved my mom and us kids more than life itself. There is absolutely nothing I can say negatively about my mom, and I don't think anyone else in the world that knows her can either. She is a true woman of God. She was the absolute best mother anyone could ask for. She was a stay-at-home mom, an excellent cook, very patient, and a superb role model. She dedicated her life to my father and us kids and was the least selfish person I know. My dad was clearly the boss of the house, but my mom was no Edith Bunker either. She would stand up to him, and I remember times when she would sleep on the couch after an argument or disagreement; however, I don't ever remember her raising her voice to my dad or any of us. She did take the hairbrush to my ass one time when I skipped school in the sixth grade, but she never had to do it again.

Both my parents are from East Tennessee and went to the University of Tennessee. They were close to their families. My dad's side was a little more eccentric. My grandfather was a very well-respected doctor, and my grandmother was heavily into politics. She would be flipping in her grave if she knew how much of a Republican I am. That side of the family tended to be a little more on the party side. There were some smokers on my dad's side and some divorces.

My mom grew up in the same town as my dad and was raised on a farm. My grandfather, on that side, was a career farmer and probably the greatest man who ever lived. He built all of his houses and barns, was a very skilled artist, and was the most patient man I have ever known. I never saw him lose his temper, ever. I would spend every summer helping on the farm, and those are my fondest memories. My grandmother was a second-grade schoolteacher, and she loved having me visit during the summers. She would cook the best country breakfasts and teach me some very good math and English tips. She is also the one who taught me about saving money and balancing a checkbook. She was a world traveler, a poet, a book writer, a member of many social clubs, and a member of the DAR.

THE STORY

My grandfather rarely left the farm. He had a full day, every day, with dairy cattle, beef cattle, chickens, pigs, tobacco crops, corn, wheat, hay, and all of the necessary duties that come with an almost 1,000-acre farm.

My mom's brother, Philip, was my favorite relative. He would take me under his wing every summer. He taught me how to drive a tractor and a pick-up truck (three-on-the-tree shifter) and to drink moonshine and Schlitz, before my time, I might add. Both sides of my parents' families were great, and they were always fun to visit.

I have two sisters. The youngest is my best friend, and we are very close. She has always been there for me and just feels so sorry for what I have put up with over the years. She is happily married, and she and her husband have two kids and live in the Atlanta area. The other sister, who is closest to my age, kind of went South in the ninth grade and has never really come out of the ditch. My mom cried herself to sleep many a night wondering what went wrong. She got into drugs and stealing, spent some time in prison, and has had problem after problem. I am not as close to her, as she kind of does her own thing and really does not come around much. I still love her, though. She has two kids who turned out very well despite all the obstacles they had to go through. I am very close to them and am very proud of them. I think my nephew may never get married, after seeing the dysfunctional marriage of his parents and knowing what I have gone through myself.

We moved to Los Angeles before I was a year old. I lived there about twelve years, and then my dad was transferred to Texas for his job. I have lived in Texas ever since. I graduated high school in 1980 and then started community college and then transferred to a university to achieve a bachelor's degree. It took me eleven years to get my degree, as I worked full time and went to school part time. My parents moved back to Kentucky just after I was out of high school, and I decided to stay in Texas to work and go to school. I had about three jobs, played golf, and attended college. I am probably considered a type-A personality; I don't really spend much time on the couch. I did not date much in high school or even after high school, as I worked so much and would prefer to spend time with my friends. I had one serious girlfriend for a year, but she constantly talked about marriage, and I was not at all ready to think about that! I had my own condo, always drove a nice car, traveled, and enjoyed being a young bachelor.

I met B in 1991 at a nightclub. I was playing pool with a buddy at a local pool hall, and he wanted to go to a 50's nightclub next door. I really did not want to go, as I was dressed sloppily. He convinced me to go for

THE STORY

a beer or two, so we did. I am not a forward person at all. Actually, I was rather shy around women at the time and would never take the lead in asking someone to dance. Well, B came up to me and asked me to dance. We did. Later she told me that I had great teeth and that she should know, since she is a dental hygienist. I thought she was cute, but there were no huge sparks. By this time, my buddy was ready to go, because I had a girl talking to me, and he did not. I told her we had to leave, but I enjoyed visiting with her. She said, "Hold on, let me go to the bathroom before you leave," so we waited. She came back smelling of heavy perfume and slipped a note into my back pocket. It had her name and number and said, "Call me sometime." I kept that note for about two weeks before I finally decided to call. I did not have a girlfriend at the time and thought it would probably be a good idea to see her again. I left her a voicemail on her answering machine and told her that I was going to be with a different buddy at a nightclub at the Hilton, although I can't even remember the name of the place. What do you know? She showed up. We danced and talked. She told me that she was divorced and had a three-year-old daughter. We will call her Bubba (pretty appropriate stage name). I may have given her a peck in the parking lot before we went our separate ways. I did give her my business card, so she now had my number. She called the very next day and invited me over to her apartment to eat some pizza and to meet her daughter. I kind of thought that was a little early to meet the kid. We had not even had an official date yet. I went over and we ordered pizza and watched TV, and it was fun. She continued to call and I would call her, and we started getting serious. She had many strikes against her, including being from New York, having short hair, being married before, and having a kid. Those were all traits I shied away from in the past; however, she was spunky and fun and she gave me attention, which I had not had from anyone in a while. I was always a bit shy around women, so I liked the fact that she made the move on me.

She rented an apartment and was not the world's best housekeeper. That fact kind of got on my nerves, as I am a neat freak. She had dishes piled up in the sink and allowed Bubba to eat her meals on the couch while watching TV. That was not the kind of structure I preferred, but I was still having fun and even liked the kid. After several months, I would babysit while she went out with girlfriends. She loved to country western dance, and I did not; however, I can disco with the best of them. We dated pretty seriously for six months, seeing each other almost every day when I was in town. I do travel for my job, so I was gone an average of a few days per week. On the sixth month, I gave her an engagement ring while at her parents' house in New York. I gave her a Dooney and Burke purse (she loved material things such as expensive purses), and inside the purse was her favorite perfume and a small teddy bear. I asked her to look closer at the bear. Around its neck was a string with the diamond ring. She started screaming and crying, and everyone thought it was pretty cool. I know her parents were very pleased, as they knew I was a great guy who would provide for their daughter and granddaughter.

Several weeks later, after returning from our New York trip, we started talking about a wedding date. It was at that time she told me "Oh, by the way, I am not officially divorced yet." That moment is when I should have run for the hills. I thought she had been divorced a long time. Her ex still lived in the area and was a great guy. He had a very good job and was a very good dad to Bubba. I could never get a good answer as to why she left him. I know he never beat her or cheated on her. I kind of figured out that she just got tired of him. I actually felt sorry for him, but I knew that I had nothing to do with taking her away from him. B had dated three or four other guys before me. One guy owned a dry cleaner, and she became pretty serious with him. Later I found out that he thought she was a psycho and was never so relieved to find out she had moved on to someone else. She also became very serious with a single dad that lived in a different state. He was killed in a car wreck, and she was devastated. Even years after we were married, she would start crying if she heard a song that reminded her of him. That always made me a feel a bit inferior. She also kept pictures of him in her wallet and constantly talked to his parents on the phone. Oh well, I still loved her, and I really liked the kid too.

We married in 1992 at my country club, and the kid was part of the wedding. Bubba would visit her dad almost every weekend so that B and I could be newlyweds. Later her ex was transferred to a different state, and he pretty much dropped out of the picture. Eventually he remarried. I know that Bubba loved her dad, but B did not make many attempts to make visitation easy for him.

B received a big child support check from her ex each month. Poor guy was on the hook for more than fourteen years of child support and barely had the opportunity to see her. Luckily I had a good job, so I encouraged her to save all of that money toward her college education. I did not need any of that money to help with bills and such, so recommended she start a nice growth mutual fund account for Bubba. Guess how much she socked away over those fourteen years. ZERO. I would constantly hound her to consider saving that money, and I even put down on paper some growth scenarios that would show her it could grow to over $150,000 by the time she graduated from high school. Rather, B decided to send Bubba to private school. Personally, I think private school is fine if you live in Los Angeles, Cleveland, Detroit, or some other big city where the schools may be considered substandard. We lived in a very nice suburb that was ranked among the highest school systems in the state. Well, once again, I did not get my way, and she believed private school was the best option. There was just something that bugged me about paying all of those school taxes and then paying private school tuition on top of it. I just HATE wasting money.

We continued to motor on in the marriage and then learned that she was pregnant in 1994, two years after being married. We never really had a serious discussion about kids, but she did know that I did not really want any. Bubba was enough for me, and I really loved her, even though she was starting to be a big challenge. I still remember getting the phone call, before cell phones, and I was on a business trip. I had stopped to check messages at a Holiday Inn pay phone in Grenada, Mississippi, and had an urgent message from her. When I finally reached her, she told me the news. I was trying to figure out how she was pregnant, when I thought she was on the birth control pill. She later told me that she missed one day. Wow, I am so lucky! Two years later, another one, and then two years later, another one. She finally had her tubes tied after the last one. THANK GOD for these kids, as they are the best thing that has ever happened to me and certainly the best thing that came out of this marriage. Even though I did not want kids and was a little nervous and depressed each time she became pregnant (none of them planned), I love my kids and I am a great dad.

She later told my sister that she tricked me into having those kids, and she thought it would be better for our marriage. B thought she was so tight with my sister. Blood is thicker than water, and my sister knew she was a conniving and deceptive bitch right from the start and felt sorry for me. She thought I should have married a southern belle, rather than this loud mouth, no-class Yankee. It was a real struggle for them to get along over the years at family events and vacations.

As the kids grew older and it was time for school, we found ourselves in the same private/public school debate. I told her that there was NO WAY I was going to pay for private school for my three kids, when we lived in one of the absolute best school systems in Texas. She told me that the only way she would send them to public school is if we moved to a different suburb just north of us. It was about five miles north of where we lived, and it had an even better school system; however, you paid for it. The homes were more expensive and taxes were higher. Well, she got her way again. I decided to move our family about five miles north. I figured that I could write off the taxes,

THE STORY

but could not write off the private school tuition, so I convinced myself that this move made economic sense as well. The house payment, taxes, utilities, and insurance were all higher, and I told her that I would need her help if we were to make this happen. "No problem," she offered. I never got that help.

To this day, it still amazes me that she would make a very good salary and it just seemed to disappear. She would buy groceries and kids' clothes, but that did not add up to anything close to what she was making. I may have been played for the biggest fool in the world while she hid money in coffee cans in the backyard; however, that would be considered saving, and she really did not believe in that. I paid all of the monthly bills and then had her writing checks in our joint account without looking to see what the balance was or ever making a deposit into that account. I finally had to obtain a separate account so I would not bounce checks. We also had a joint credit card, but she would never offer up any money when the bill came due, and the majority of the charges were hers. I have always believed in paying the balance in full each month. She believed in never paying in full and rather just making the minimum payment. I even showed her a magazine article that would tell the story of how many years it takes to pay off a $5,000 credit card balance if you make only the minimum payment. It did not faze her. Rather, she would just open a new credit card account behind my back, once the first one was maxed out. What the hell was she spending all of this money on? It was certainly not the house payment, insurance, taxes, utilities, car payment, home maintenance, home furnishings, travel, or the restaurants we frequented. I picked up the tab on all of those things. She was the worst manager of money I have ever seen, and I was starting to develop some resentment.

Her parents were simple blue-collar folks, but at least they believed in investing and putting away for retirement. B just had a special gene in her DNA makeup that prevented her from giving a damn about saving for the future or putting money away for kids' college education. She would even tell people that you just gotta "LIVE FOR THE DAY." Maybe because she had the old boyfriend, who died in a car crash, she felt like it was better just to spend and enjoy. I asked her, "What happens if Armageddon does not happen, and we live to ninety-five years old?" Wouldn't it be nice to have some money in the bank to supplement Social Security, if it is even around? She just had a blank look on her face.

I come from a family of long livers. My grandmother, the one who taught me about saving, lived to ninety-nine. I had an aunt who was 106 and an uncle who was 103.

THE STORY

I understand that the separation of finances is a form of marital separation, and it pained me to do it; however, I had to take some measures, as she was going to run me into the poor house.

We continued to go to church, and the pastor would even preach about debt and how it can lead to depression and it is not biblical to be a slave to debt. I honestly think she would just daydream, as nothing the pastor talked about would faze her. She became more and more deceptive in opening charge accounts and even stealing checks that were made out to me for expense reports or insurance refunds, etc. She truly did live for the day. Did she not think I would ever find out about an $800 expense check that was sent to me, and she cashed it? I spent several hours on the phone with my company and the bank trying to clear up how their records showed the check had been cashed, yet I never received it. After some investigation and seeing a copy of the back of the check, it showed that she had endorsed it and taken cash. What a waste of time and an embarrassment that I had a wife who would do this! This happened on several occasions. It got to the point of where I would ask her if she had a check of mine, if a certain amount of time went by in waiting for a check that I was counting on. One time she said, "Oh yes, I received it a few weeks ago and meant to give it to you," as she pulled it out from underneath her stainless steel tray of perfumes. We all know that she was trying to scam that check and was just giving it some time to see if I brought it up before maliciously cashing it for herself.

In 2004, my heart was truly broken. Even with all of the stupid money issues she had, I still loved her. She was my wife, and I honestly believed in FOR BETTER OR WORSE, and just continued to pray that she would someday see the light and get on board with me and allow me to be the spiritual and financial leader of our home, but then I learned she was having an affair. I bought a Radio Shack phone recorder so that I could find out what was going on in my house while I was out of town. I went to these measures not because I was concerned about my wife's unfaithfulness, but because I had a fifteen-year-old stepdaughter who was involving herself in drinking, drugs, tattoos, piercings, and sex parties. Bubba had been going in the wrong direction since about eighth grade, and that was when our relationship soured. I had no authority over her and B would not give it to me. Rather, she would hide things from me and not ever hold Bubba accountable for anything. I did not even try hard, but would learn of many things that would be the most disappointing thing a parent can learn about their child. Sure enough, Bubba was calling friends to take her to get her tongue pierced, so that told me she must have had a fake ID.

As a bonus, I found out my wife was having a relationship with an older single guy from our church. He was a known womanizer. As soon as I left town, they would start planning their get-togethers. When I heard this information on the recording, I honestly went straight to the bathroom at my office and threw up. I lost weight and was sick about it. I wanted to divorce her SO MUCH. I was not going to leave her, though, as I had small kids. My son was only four at the time, and I was not about to leave him and allow him to be raised by some redneck that she would surely marry soon after a divorce. I was truly TRAPPED. I hated what she did to me but learned to keep it bottled up. I even went to a Christian counselor for some help. No matter how miserable I was with certain aspects of our marriage, I NEVER had an affair and NEVER would. Anyone who knows me knows that I would not do that. This newfound information certainly put more stress on our marriage, and my resentment continued to grow.

There was a time, several months later, that she may have actually had some remorse. She got back into church and even went to the altar to rededicate her life to the Lord. She later participated in a water baptism. I was very happy about this and learned to forgive her. We talked about the recordings only one time, and I did not bring it up every time I became angry at her. It was a very sad and hurtful event to me, and I tried the best I could to put it out of my mind, which is not really possible. You cannot simply hit a reset button to your brain to clear out this information. Things went well for a while since her new rebirth. I wanted to be happily married to B, and we even participated in some marriage counseling classes at our church. We would even pray together at night, which is a surefire way to strengthen a marriage. I tried to get her into some financial planning and money management courses at our church, but she resisted. She started slipping back into running up credit card debt and going out with a girlfriend and staying out very late. I suspected she was possibly being promiscuous again, but I did not even confront her. I was happy to be there for my kids. Later I found out there were other guys as well. It was not long until I was back being miserable, but still would not leave her. Being a good dad to my kids was more important than my own happiness. I had several friends tell me that I should not have to put up with that and should initiate a divorce. One friend would joke that I could never pull the trigger, as I was too cheap and did not want to give her a big chunk of my money. I know that I am not an easily influenced person, as I did not listen to anyone. I knew that I wanted to be there for my kids, and I also knew that B was not the person I saw myself with at seventy-five years old sitting on a front porch swing holding hands and drinking coffee; however, I felt TRAPPED.

THE STORY

While all of this was going on, we continued to have more problems with Bubba. She had no rules. I took the car away from her when I learned she had a tattoo as a minor and would not tell me where she got it. The next week, B bought her a brand-new car. I took her cell phone away when I learned that she had posted pictures of herself naked on some website. B got her a new, better cell phone and started paying for her plan. I had no power in the house, and they continued to mow me over at every turn.

B threw a big beer keg party for Bubba and a bunch of her friends when they were seventeen years old. I was out of town when this occurred. When I found out, I was furious. I complained that we could have been set up for a huge lawsuit if someone found out we had served alcohol to minors or if someone had left that party and been in a car accident. To this day, she still says she would do it again, as she would rather have them drinking at home than somewhere else. This logic is the sign of someone with a low IQ. I can't understand how she thinks it is OK to contribute to minors (minors who are drinking four years before their time). How about raising Bubba the way my dad raised me? He said that I had better not drink alcohol, PERIOD, and if I did, my life would change. B was more of a friend to Bubba than a mother. She prided herself in being the cool mom. Bubba and her friends would call her Madre. Once Bubba was in college, B would leave the rest of us for days at a time to go visit her. I would see the Facebook pictures of her partying it up with the eighteen and nineteen year olds.

Bubba received a DWI her first year of college. She also was having sex with anything that could fog a mirror. She got into pot, mushrooms, and who knows what else? I would pray hard every night that my three kids did not turn out like Bubba. I had to be there for them. Bubba had no male role model in her life, as B removed me from having any authority, and they avoided her real dad at all costs, which was sad, to me.

In 2008, B and my oldest daughter (about thirteen) started to gang up on me in regard to buying a new house. The 2,777 square feet we had was just not enough, and it was surely one of the smaller homes in the affluent area we lived in. They worked me hard for months and months. It would really be nice to have a guest room, a game room, an office, and much more square footage in a different neighborhood so that we could live by many of the professional athletes and other celebrities that lived in our town. I resisted for a while and then finally caved in and agreed to start looking around. Why was I such a pussy? I loved the home we were in and thought we would live there forever. It was only about two times the size of the house that I grew up in and about three times the size of her parents' home in New York; however, a part of me thought it may be a good time to do this, since interest rates were low and I could move my office into the house if we had the extra room. I thought it would be fun to walk about twenty steps into my office and wear my underwear to do my morning sales conference call. In addition, this would save me the monthly rent that I was paying for an office nearby. I told them we would not do anything until we have listed and sold our current house. Well, our home sold in two days, and then we were panicked to find a home. Luckily, the guy who bought our house to allowed us to rent it back for two months.

I had a budget in mind of about $600,000 or under and actually found a very nice home that would have had all the things we were looking for. B told me of a home in a different prestigious neighborhood that was for sale. I knew about this subdivision. Those were million-dollar homes. She said the real estate agent told her this couple was desperate to sell and it didn't hurt to look. I agreed. Once I saw the house, there was no comparison. I loved it too, but it was about $200,000 over my budget. We were able to talk the couple down a bit, but I told B that I would need her help if we were to buy this home. I have always prided myself in living below my means, but we would not be exercising that rule. This home was 5,500 square feet and the taxes were going to double from what we had been paying.

The utilities and maintenance were sure to go up as well. This castle had THREE air conditioning units. I told her that I could afford the higher house payment and utilities as long as she could pay the property taxes, which were about $17,000 per year. She agreed, as she was almost in tears needing this house. This is the house that would make her happy. The real estate agents were right there and witnessed our agreement for her to save money in order to pay the taxes. Am I stupid? Why did I think she would help with the taxes? This was the lady who would steal my checks and open credit card accounts behind my back. She never saved a dime toward the taxes that were due that first year and for any of the other three years that we were there. I would sell stock each year in order to pay the taxes. I was tricked again and played for a fool, but she had her big house to show off, so that she would pretend to be some big shot. Buying this house was one of the biggest mistakes I have ever made. I even borrowed $100,000 from my mom in order to keep the loan amount below a jumbo. My mom even got shafted in the end when B denied it was a loan and claimed it was a gift. Does she even have a conscience at all? She is very happy to screw anyone who can benefit her.

I have to admit I loved the house, and the kids seemed very happy there. My two youngest would walk down a private path to their elementary school, and

THE STORY

my oldest would catch a bus right out front to her middle school. I loved having my office at the house and would often take breaks to do some yard work or service the pool. We had one of the best yards in the neighborhood (one-half-acre lot), and our pool was spotless. We also had a guest room for friends and family to use when they came to town. We had a game room with a pool table, Ping-Pong and a Wii. I would choke on the payment, utilities, and taxes, but did enjoy the very nice custom home. I did not need it but was having fun with it. I became very close to my next-door neighbors, and we kind of had a yard contest.

B became more and more strange. She would often get angry while driving and just become very short with people. She was starting to get a reputation in the area as a hothead. She would chew people out, honk her horn, flip drivers off, etc. She chased a neighbor girl down the street with a shovel in her hand, and the parents went to the police about it. It became embarrassing to be married to her. When my fifteen-year-old and a few other girls did not make the cheerleading squad (for lack of skills), she spearheaded a petition to have them reconsidered and really made some waves. My fifteen-year-old did not even want to be on the team, but B insisted. The principal of the school had to get involved, and eventually B did not get her way. She also sued a guy whose dog bit Bubba's dog while

I WAS TRAPPED IN A MISERABLE MARRIAGE AND SCREWED BY THE TERRIBLE SYSTEM!

B was walking it. She lost that case and just seemed to be frustrated with other folks. She had about forty different jobs while being married to me, so I already knew that she could not get along with others, especially woman. She hated the women in the office and would quit a job just because she couldn't get along with someone.

I believe she found her new love of power when she sued a dentist that she worked for. B worked for an older dentist that was partially crippled. He was hit by a car years before and had some very noticeable disabilities. She came home from work one day and told me that she was going to quit because he sexually harassed her. First of all, I could not believe it. This guy was married and had kids in college and seemed like the nicest guy you would ever meet. She claimed that she was cleaning his teeth and he reached out and tried to touch her boob. She sure did not seem too shaken up. Anyway, I helped her type a letter saying she was going to resign and asking for a couple months' severance pay. The next thing I know, she had hired some ambulance-chaser law firm that specialized in sexual harassment. She was going for the jugular and would ruin his practice if he did not pay. She went to a counselor for her mental anguish, probably recommended by her lawyer to set the stage for the big kill. Later she extorted $33,000 out of the dentist as a settlement to keep the case out of court and save his practice from the negative publicity. I felt so sorry for this guy. Would you believe that one of B's friends later told me that they had been drinking wine and doing nitrous shots after work? I can't prove it, but I sure believe it was a setup. Getting a check from his practice made her feel very powerful, and she became a lover of attorneys.

B was on Prozac for years and maybe needed to be put back on it. She was never officially diagnosed with anything, and I was surprised that her ob-gyn would give her a prescription for it just because she said she had the blues. I did not like her on Prozac, as it may not have been the right medication and it made her not give a shit about anything. In my opinion, she may be bipolar. I'm not sure if we will ever know, because in her opinion, she was just normal as can be and everyone else had the issues.

She really had NO friends. She had very short-term friends, but no one that she was close to. She was famous for alienating people. She was too loud and opinionated, and she hated you forever if you disagree with her on something.

I, on the other hand, had many friends. I had about ten of them set to testify if we had gone to trial for a custody issue. These were folks that had known B and me for years and were ready to testify that they could not believe what I had to put up with. Many of my friends felt sorry for me for the total lack of respect she showed me.

We rarely went out with other couples, and toward the end, my friends would not even come over to the house if they knew she was there. It was embarrassing to go out to dinner with her, as she would always find something wrong with her meal and loved to complain. I am opposite of that. If someone put mustard on my hamburger, I would wipe it off rather than send it back, and I HATE mustard! She would complain about anything, make a scene, and enjoy it. She knew it made me uncomfortable, but relished that.

THE FILING

I knew things were not going well in our marriage. She moved Bubba in for the summer, even though her and her ex-husband were paying for her apartment in her college town five hours away. I was totally against this as we couldn't get along and that was the laziest kid I had even known. I did not want her sleeping in and lying out by the pool all summer while I worked out of the house. I suggested she stay at her apartment during summer break and GET A JOB. Well, I was overruled, and she moved in, along with her one-hundred-pound chocolate Lab. We already had a Lab of our own, also against my wishes. One morning her dog was lying in the middle of our leather couch, and I proceeded to take the cushions off and store them at a friend's house for the summer visit. B thought that was the weirdest thing she had ever seen in her life and accused me of being some sort of psycho. I reminded her that I was the one who paid $5,000 for that couch, and I didn't want some undisciplined dog lying on the damn couch. I told her she could go out a buy a couch for that dog if she wished, but it was not going to destroy the one we had. That damn dog would walk through the flowerbeds, jump in the pool, and just generally trash the place; however, I stayed calm and put up with it. Why? Because I was trapped.

B would go out all the time and stay until the very early hours of the morning. There were times when she did not even come home. Most husbands would have a cow and probably confront their wives. I just allowed it to happen, as I really did not care for her any longer. I was there for my kids, thank God. She would often comment about all of my happy hours. I did like to meet friends for a beer now and then, and that usually consisted of two or three beers and I was home by 6:30. B would not even get started until about 10:00 at night and then would come stumbling home drunk, if she even came home. I started making notes of her being out of the house, in case I ever needed them. I felt like the end might be near, even though I was not going to pull the trigger. We could not get along or agree on anything. All the while, I had more and more resentment building for her sticking me with all of the new higher bills in our home and the constant deceit.

B and the three kids left the house one morning in 2011 to go to their doctor appointments. I was working

THE FILING

at my desk when I saw a man walking toward the front door with a clipboard. I thought he looked like a process server. I did not answer the door. I figured I would not be so easy to be served a divorce notice. I was leaving town the next day for a week and decided to get the heck out right then. He rang the doorbell and called the home phone number, and I ignored him. I started packing the stuff that I would need for the business trip and continued working. I threw all my stuff over the backyard fence into my neighbor's yard. I knocked on her door, and she let me in so that I could explain what was going on. She walked out to the mailbox to pretend to check her mail. The man with the clipboard stopped her and said, "Do you know where J. Golf is?" She said that she did not and asked if there was anything she could help him with. He said he was a process server and needed to get some papers to Mr. Golf. It was apparent that I was home, as my car was out front and the garden hose was running to soak some big trees, because of the hot summer we had been having. I was spying on him out her front window and noticed him using his cell phone. He was evidently in contact with B and trying to figure out why I would not answer the door.

Suddenly my cell phone rang. It was B. She said she just called me to determine what I was doing. I acted like everything was fine and told her that my buddy Ken came by to pick me up and we went for lunch.

◄ I WAS TRAPPED IN A MISERABLE MARRIAGE AND SCREWED BY THE TERRIBLE SYSTEM!

She asked where we went. I told her Boomer Jack's, a local place I liked about five miles away. The next thing I saw was the process server answered his phone and wrote something down. Obviously B told him where I supposedly was. It was really going to give her pleasure to have me served in public! As soon as he got in his car and drove off, I ran outside, turned the hose off, and backed my car into my neighbor's driveway, to load my things. My flight did not leave until the next day, but I decided to check into the La Quinta Inn near the airport to stay out of the house.

I went to my buddy's house to review all the new developments and have someone to talk to. I was not really surprised that the divorce might be coming down; however, I was a little shocked that she pulled the trigger, since she had a life of EASY STREET. I did not think she would put our younger kids through a divorce from their father. She already did it once to Bubba. Her pattern repeated itself.

I instantly hired a private detective to see if she was having an affair. On the second day, he confirmed that she was indeed having an affair with "The Loser." That is how I will refer to the new boyfriend, and it is very appropriate. Later I learned that he had been married three times and had five daughters from all those marriages. He was a renter, had been sued more than once, and had multiple DWI's. In addition, I could not verify that he actually had a job, or at least a real job. He often told my kids that he was a millionaire. I am sure that was what impressed B from the beginning, if he gave her that kind of sales pitch. They would go out to eat and drink and then go back to his condo. She would leave the kids at home until the very late hours of the night and then stumble home drunk. After reviewing cell phone bills provided during discovery, I determined that she had been seeing this guy for about six months, which explained all those late nights out. Many times she would claim to be going out with one of her girlfriends; however, when I reviewed the phone bills, she would not have one phone call to that girlfriend, but many to The Loser. I am sure The Loser was helping coach her, since he had been through the process so many times and was probably going to relish the fact that some other guy was about to get screwed. In addition, who knows what kind of lies B told him about me? She was a known liar. She lied in our temporary-orders court date about things that would later screw me, and I had nothing I could do about it. Have you heard the saying that nice guys finish last?

Two weeks prior to filing for divorce, she took $17,000 out of our HELOC (home equity line of credit) account. It was an account that we opened to pay off some land we owned in North Carolina, to obtain a better interest rate. I made all the payments on this loan and had actually gotten it paid down to about $45,000 from the original $75,000. I always made additional principal payments rather than just the minimum interest amount that was required. She had nothing to do with this account, but she had to co-sign, since her name was on the mortgage. Well, she knew her name was on that account, and she knew we had room to borrow more against it. She used that $17,000 to pay $12,000 down on a brand new Camaro for my sixteen-year-old and the other $5,000 was to open a retainer with her divorce attorney. She actually bought a brand new $30,000 rear-wheel-drive racecar for my daughter who had just obtained her driver's license. The funniest part of it all was that they did not ask me or consult me. They actually hid it down the street when I was in town and then parked it in the garage when I was out of town. She knew her surprise filing was coming up, and they just had to keep the car a secret until then. What makes me very sad is that my sixteen-year-old was part of the deception. She later cried about it when she knew that I found out. She truly felt sorry that they did this behind my back. My daughter did not even want a new Camaro. She would have been thrilled with a used Chrysler 300 and would ooh and ahh about them when she saw one. I thought it was funny, because that car reminded me more of something that an old salesman would drive. Anyway, you can buy a six or seven year old model for about $5,000, and that probably would have been better for a new teen driver. Guess what. She ended up totaling the Camaro.

THE FILING

B also cleaned out the joint checking account. Even though it was a joint account, she had not made a deposit into that account in years. I kept it open in order to have our HELOC loan payment drafted each month, in order to obtain a lower interest rate. Luckily she could not clean out my other checking account that I used for my payroll deposits and to pay all my other monthly bills such as the house payment, utilities, insurance, etc. She also moved her jewelry, guns, come crystal, clothes, and even her vibrator out of the house.

The night of the filing, from my La Quinta Hotel room, I e-mailed B to let her know that I knew what was going on. As much as I could not stand the woman, I still wanted to be there for my kids. I honestly think she believed I was planning to file and she wanted to beat me to it. I made three attempts to communicate with her about what we were about to go through and had NO response. She was already listening to her attorneys, I'm sure. If she truly wanted out of the marriage, then I begged to work up an agreement between ourselves rather than getting a bunch of attorneys involved who would likely milk us. I could not imagine spending thousands of dollars on bottom feeders that were famous for running the clock and extending things time and time again. That type of attorney reminded me of when I went to a topless bar for my bachelor party, and the dancers acted like they were your absolute best friend, as long as you were feeding them cash. Once the cash dried up, they vanished.

I knew there were good attorneys in the world. Hell, there are probably some good car salesmen too, but they do have a stereotype for a reason

I did not know what to do next, so I hired an attorney while out of town on my business trip. I did not even know of a divorce attorney, so I called a big national chain that often advertised as a pro-dad firm. This was a big mistake. I transferred the balance of what we had available in our HELOC account, in order to get them started. I was proud to tell B that I now had a lawyer and her lawyer could just serve the papers to him. I did not look forward to coming back in town and having a process server waiting for me when I got off the plane or when I was walking up my front-door step. This was the beginning of a miserable process that would last more than fourteen months and rape me of a huge chunk of my years of savings.

I confirmed that my attorney had indeed received the petition. B was filing for irreconcilable differences. While I was gone, she had THE DISCUSSION with the kids. The middle daughter (fourteen) was in shock and was basically hyperventilating about this news. My son (eleven) was also crying, and my oldest daughter

THE FILING

(sixteen) knew we did not get along and thought it would be best. She actually thought it was pretty cool, since most of her friends' parents were divorced and that it was fun having two houses to go back and forth between. I just love sixteen-year-olds. They have no clue about anything, just as long as their life is going OK.

I proudly returned home from my business trip and was not about to stay at a hotel again. After all, I was not the adulterer or the one who wanted to break up the family. She could get her ass out of the house and move in with The Loser. I came home, changed the sheets in the bed, and went to bed that night. She stayed on the couch (oh yes, I did end up putting the cushions back on). She did not know I had the private eye and had a lot of information on her. She told me that she and the kids (including Bubba) were leaving the next day to visit her family In New York and would be gone about ten days. I was absolutely fine with that, as the kids needed a good vacation before returning to school anyway. This all took place during summer break. She had The Loser's daughter (one of five from three different wives) take them to the airport.

I met with my newly hired attorney to come up with our counter petition, which included charges of adultery and cruelty in a marriage. The attorney said I had a great chance to get a disproportionate share of our resources, because of the evidence I had compiled. I was feeling pretty good about everything.

While they were gone, I went through her closet (much messier and cluttered than mine) and found a huge stash of marijuana, pipes, bongs, and some stuff that I am not even sure what it would be used for. I confiscated these items and made sure to notify my attorney about them. I knew that she used drugs before we were married but was not aware that she was using them again. I figured her Prozac and booze and other painkillers that she often took constituted the extent of her habit. Was she a possible drug dealer that I was living with?

Several weeks later, I received a notice that a temporary hearing date was set. Evidently this is standard practice, and trust me, THIS WAS AN IMPORTANT DATE. This was where all orders were established while the process dragged on; a process I thought might last a couple months. Surely we could agree to dissolve the marriage and go our separate ways. AM I STUPID? I forgot who I was dealing with.

At the temporary hearing, I was convinced to move out, since only one of us could stay in the house with the kids, and I traveled for a living. I had to be out that night but could continue to use my home office from the hours of 8:30 to 4:00 each day. That arrangement would be good for only three weeks, at which time I had to move my office out of the house too and give her exclusive use of the home. After the hearing, I called one of my best friends and old neighbors to see if I could move in for a couple of weeks while I come up with a plan. Dave and his wife were more than willing to help me. I actually introduced them to each other about nine years earlier, after they had both gone through divorces. They are probably the happiest couple I know.

Dave was sick about what was going on in my situation, and they were great people to talk to when I was in town. I really did not want to rent an apartment. I don't want to sound like a snob, but I have never rented an apartment in my life, and I figured the divorce process would be over in a very short time and I would buy a condo or smaller home near my kids. Can you believe that the possible two-week stay turned into more than a YEAR? Thank God for the two of them for taking me in. They never hinted once that they might be sick of me. I used an air mattress in their media room and had use of their sixty-inch flat screen TV so that I could watch Bill O'Reilly every night before going to bed, a tradition for me. I hope to be on the Bill O'Reilly program promoting my book someday...ha ha.

I WAS TRAPPED IN A MISERABLE MARRIAGE AND SCREWED BY THE TERRIBLE SYSTEM!

Dave's wife was great. She would constantly call me to make sure I was coming home for dinner, and she even took pleasure in doing my laundry. They are truly from God, and I can never repay them for what they did. They even threw me a fiftieth birthday party, and we had a huge turnout. They had catered fajitas and mango daiquiris, beer, cake, and more. My kids came too, and it was a blast. Everyone brought gifts, even though we told them not to. I am sure they all felt sorry for me. Anyway, I obtained a very large stash of my favorite scotch and bourbon and many starter items for a home that many knew I would soon need. Friends are great, and I am blessed to have good ones.

I really got screwed at the temporary orders hearing. I had a terrible attorney who was more concerned with getting to his next client than helping me make life-changing decisions. I agreed to pay the house payment, the taxes, the insurance, half of the Camaro payments, and the maximum amount of child support that anyone had to pay in Texas. Bill Gates would not pay more than I did.

In Texas there is a formula based on a maximum of $7,500 per month. For three kids, you pay 30% of that amount, so that ends up being $2,250. When you add all the items up that I was paying monthly, plus throw in the attorney fees, I was going BACKWARDS every single month; however, I thought it would last only a

THE FILING

month or two. We agreed to these temporary orders rather than actually seeing the judge, in order to let him determine what was best and fair. To this day, I could kick myself hard. I can't believe I could have done any worse by seeing the judge.

We also agreed to let me continue coming over to do the yard work and clean the pool, in order to save money and to keep up with my high standards for perfection. I did not want someone else doing my yard work, as he would not be as picky and wouldn't know where all the sprinkler heads were located, and they could be damaged. I would have access to both garages to access lawn equipment and pool chemicals, so I could be a personal slave to the bitch who was living in my house, the house I was still paying for but could not go in. I joked with friends and customers that I had owned five houses in my lifetime. All five of them were 100% the result of the money I had saved to get into those homes, and now I was living on a FU_ _ _ _ _ air mattress at a friend's house. Something was wrong with that picture. I did travel often for my job, so when I was not on the air mattress, I would stay at a very nice Marriott.

The worst part about being out of the house was the separation from the kids. I loved nothing more than returning to town to see my kids and get a hug from them. My middle daughter really missed me when I traveled and would even cry when I packed my suitcase. She called me often and told me that "All Mom does is scream the whole time," and that comment broke my heart. She was a very sensitive kid who needed lots of love. I did not want her to grow up my like my black-sheep sister who was also a middle child. My daughter wrote me a note once that told me how much she missed me when I was out of town and that I was the best dad she could ever have prayed for. I loved that note and kept it in my work binder. Later, that note disappeared along with other personal notes. I have a feeling I know who discarded them while snooping through my things. B hated the thought of me possessing anything that actually made me look good. She even went through my Bible and threw away some very personal notes I had saved from friends who were encouraging me because of the situation I was in. I can't prove who took those notes and discarded them, but I have a sneaking suspicion that it could be the same person who confiscated and cashed my checks. Prozac can make you do funny things, you know.

The discovery process started. The discovery process is where you spend hours printing out all your investments, payroll, banking, credit card, and phone information as well as any other statement that is attached to your life. You then give those to your attorney, and they spend hours going through and

THE FILING

organizing them so they can bill the shit out of you. The most amazing part is that they ask for this information time and time again as the months wear on. They constantly want updated statements. We finally had a court date set in May. That was good news to me, because the longest this misery could possibly last was until May, if we were not able to settle sooner. Well, guess what. She fired her attorney and then hired a new one. The new one was a known bloodsucker in our area and was famous for running the clock until there were no more resources. I honestly think her first attorney may have fired her, as he probably could not talk any sense into her. Nonetheless, the change proved to be very costly to our estate. The new bottom feeder applied for an extension with the court, as he needed more time to conduct discovery and become familiar with the case. I had been on a bad luck roll, and it continued. The extension was granted, and he had five more months to run the clock on us.

I think I had at least three more discovery requests during this time and the attorneys just kept billing me for the time it took to go through all of this paperwork. I was getting monthly attorney bills for $7,000 to $9,000 EACH MONTH! Let me explain something to you. I net about $3,200 in each paycheck (twice per month) and I was paying the house payment of $2,700, property taxes that are about $1,500 per month, child support of $2,250 per month, and having to pay my own living expenses. You don't have to be a gifted math wizard to understand that I was going backwards each month. I continued to sell stock all along the way.

The BEST part of the whole story is that about eight months into it, I found out the attorney was coming after me for HER attorney fees, as she had never paid anyone a dime. Everyone I knew told me that I would not be responsible for her attorney fees. I was. We went to court and the judge made me sell the rest of my taxable mutual funds to pay her attorneys, since she did not have any money. I honestly thought that day in court was a bad dream or that I was on *Candid Camera*. Was this America? She had the affair, she wanted the divorce, she wanted the new attorney and extension, but she was not responsible for having to pay anything. It was as if her years of non-saving were being rewarded. Poor people's divorces go so much faster and probably have much less drama and anger. I was basically financing the entire process that I did not even want a part of.

She was in no hurry to move the process along, as the temporary orders were in her favor. She was getting a big fat child support check from me, and she had a free house to live in with me not being allowed to step foot on the property. Thank God that I am stable and well adjusted, as I can sure see how people walk into courthouses and start shooting. The entire process can surely throw people over the cliff of going crazy if they are teetering on a nervous breakdown.

I continued to attend church, pray, and work out to relieve stress and help me keep my sanity. In Fort Worth there was a case years ago wherein a guy named George Lott walked into the courtroom and started shooting at his ex-wife, the judge, and the attorneys. I remember thinking what a disturbed man that must have been. I can honestly say that he was probably at his wit's end with the system. I consider myself a strong Christian and would never condone something like that, but I can honestly say that I understand what he was probably going through. The guy simply had enough. Because of that situation, you now have to walk through metal detectors at the courthouse, just like the airport.

At the temporary hearing, we agreed that I would continue to do the yard work and service the pool to save our estate money, and we all knew what a perfectionist I was with both. I had to give her twenty-four hours' notice before coming over.

One time I sent her the e-mail to explain I was coming over to do the yard and she said, "No, don't worry about it."

I said "No, I am coming to do the yard, as it has been a week and it needs mowing and I am leaving town the next day."

She said, "No thanks. Please don't come."

That whack job was not going to tell me when the yard needed mowing, so I went over anyway. I opened the garage door and started up the edger and began work. By the way, The Loser was over there. When I went back to the garage to return the edger and pull out the mower, someone had closed the garage door. I went back to my car to get the opener. When I tried to open it this time, it got hung up about two feet off the ground. I could see a big push broom dangling from the side when I tried and tried to open the door. It would go up about two feet and then close. I crawled under the two-foot opening to discover her and The Loser had shoved the broom between the door and the steel track to keep the door from opening. Little to their surprise, I yanked the broom out, opened the door, and proceeded to mow. Ten minutes into my mowing, a local police officer pulled up in front of our home. I thought surely he could not be there for me. He gave me the time-out signal, so I shut down the mower. He asked, "What are you doing?"

I explained, "Mowing my yard."

He asked if I lived here.

I said, "This is my home, and I have made every single mortgage payment since I purchased it."

He asked to see my driver's license and said he would go talk to B. I asked if I could mow while he was in there, and he said yes. Fifteen minutes later, he came out, so I shut down my mower again. He returned my driver's license and told me that he told her that I was allowed to be there and there was really nothing he could do. I told him that she was crazy; he smiled and said, "GOOD LUCK." My middle daughter came home while all of this was going on and started crying. She could not figure out why her mom would call the police on me for mowing the yard. This was the yard of the house that I purchased for my family.

The next day I fired off an e-mail and explained I would no longer be mowing the yard or servicing the pool and that she could go to the expense of having those services provided. I was furious that the bitch thought she could call the police on me because she told me not to mow the yard so she and The Loser could have some time alone in my house. She was on the world's biggest power trip.

Later she sent me a month's worth of bills for the mowing and pool service, and I basically told her to shove it where the sun did not shine. I sent her an e-mail asking her who three gentlemen were. I had the names of three guys, and I asked her how she was connected to them. I went through her phone bills and found phone numbers that she had called time and time again. Some of those calls were at very late hours of the night and many were when I was out of town. I called those numbers to see who answered. All three of them were guys' voices. I called from my fax machine so they could not call right back and ask who I was. I provided their phone numbers to my private detective, and he provided their names. She would never answer me as to who they were. We were now talking about as many as five possible affairs.

My friend's wife was in a dentist chair one day getting her teeth cleaned. B's name came up and the hygienist said she knew her. She said that she is the one who had an affair with a dentist. My friend never told me this until he knew B had filed for divorce. He did not want me to know about it, since it came from a third party and he had no proof. Anyway, it all makes sense now. It was a pattern, and it kept repeating itself.

The Camaro was another sore spot. It was bad enough that she bought the car two weeks prior to filing for divorce with a down payment that she basically stole. She also lied about the payment, I later found out. She told the court that it was $450 per month and I agreed to pay half. I paid my $225 per month for about the first six months and then noticed in her discovery that the payment amount was actually only $325. She screwed me again. I stopped paying it and sent her several notes explaining that I needed to see her proof of payments and the payment coupon so that I could verify the correct car payment. I even told her that I had reason to believe she lied about the payment amount. My notes fell on deaf ears and she would never respond. Several months later I was served papers at my son's football practice that said I was in contempt of court for failure to pay bills that were part of our temporary orders. In this filing, she claims I was behind in paying the Camaro payment, maintenance bills for the house, and a whole bunch of other invoices for work she had done in the house, including having all of the locks changed, carpet cleaning, light bulb replacement, sprinkler repairs, repair of the grill, and garage-door work. First of all, she changed the locks to keep me out. Do you really think I want to pay for that? She had the carpet cleaned and she was totally aware that I own a carpet-cleaning machine and used to clean carpets for a living. She hired someone to change a $3.00 sprinkler head that I could have done myself, had she asked. The outdoor grill never worked since we moved in. I chose to light it by hand rather than pay to have the auto starters replaced. Well, once I was out, she thought it would be a good idea to have those repaired so that she and The

I WAS TRAPPED IN A MISERABLE MARRIAGE AND SCREWED BY THE TERRIBLE SYSTEM!

Loser could grill steaks and use the hot tub and pool. The garage door needed repairs because she shoved a broom in the track to keep me out. In my opinion, I did not owe any of this crap and was not planning to pay her. My attorney, expensive attorney, told me that I was not obligated to pay any maintenance items, but I did need to get current on the car payment. I said, "Excuse me? I have overpaid as it is, since she lied about the payment." She said it did not matter that she lied, because we both agreed to pay $225 per month toward the car. Even though she has never produced proof of what the actual payment was or when it was due, I was still supposed to continue paying? My attorney told me that if I was found in contempt, I could go to jail. I wrote a big check to pay that amount. I thought it was another bad dream. How the hell could I go to jail when I had never done anything worse than drive a little over the speed limit? I really question the justice system in this country sometimes. I know it is by far the best place in the world to live, but I kind of like the justice system in some Middle East countries where they behead wives for having affairs. Sorry, I guess that does not sound very Christ-like.

HAZEL

Oh my god, I have not written in about two weeks, and my life has taken a tremendously positive turn. I have met someone named Hazel who is from God. I was not looking and she was not looking, but we have sure hit it off. I honestly believe this is the woman I will be with for the rest of my life. She is so opposite of what I had with B. She is calm, classy, reserved, and very caring. She loves going to church and honestly makes me feel so good about myself. I certainly loved B at one time, but it was nothing like this. Hazel hates to be away from me and e-mails and calls me all the time. That would usually be a turnoff, as I don't like to be too smothered; however, I just love it. I am in Tulsa right now, and she must have e-mailed me thirty times yesterday with just little short notes about how much she likes me and how much she cares about me. I have NEVER had this before. And get this, she likes to save money! I am very excited about the direction this is going.

I WAS TRAPPED IN A MISERABLE MARRIAGE AND SCREWED BY THE TERRIBLE SYSTEM!

Back to the court system. In my county, there is something like 12,000 divorces a year and there are only four judges. I have determined they don't give a damn about you or your circumstances or any of the details. They are just trying to push these cases through the system and keep their dockets from backing up too much. I NEVER was given an opportunity to tell my side of the story on anything. I would get to tell my story if we had gone to trial, but that would have cost another $40,000, and guess who would be on the hook for that. I have already exhausted all of my taxable savings, and if I started dipping into IRAs, that would result in taxes and penalties. This entire process just sucks. I really wish I had just represented myself. I got absolutely nowhere with my expensive attorney. I know they invested time on my case by organizing all of the discovery paperwork that I would spend hours retrieving time and time again; however, I did not need them for that. I could have supplied that directly to B's attorney. I would have saved thousands and thousands by going this route.

HER DEPOSITION

We deposed B several months into the process. This was the only part of the entire process that I felt went my way. My attorney was very good at crafting her questions and making B look like a total idiot. I gave my attorney a list of questions to ask her, and she used some of them and some she did not. She also designed some of her own questions. The very first question she asked her was if she had ever had an abortion. I thought that question was kind of odd, as I did not have it listed and did not really know why it would matter. In addition, I knew that B did not believe in abortion. Well, to my surprise she answered yes. When my attorney asked her for a year that it occurred, B told her it was probably about 1983. She must have been knocked up in high school, and I did not even know it. I later asked why she asked this question and if she had known this fact about B. She said she hadn't known, but that she liked to start a deposition with a shock question. She then asked her if she knew a gentleman by the name of L.S. (abbreviated). She answered yes, we knew him from church. She asked if she had ever had sex with L.S. There was a long silence. She asked the same question again, and it was followed by more silence. B's attorney was curiously looking at her and wondering if she was going to answer at all. My attorney said, "Have you had sex with L.S.? That means oral sex or intercourse. What is your answer to the court?" More silence, and I actually almost felt sorry for her. I think B had a lot of things going through her mind, and she did not want to get caught in a lie.

She finally answered, "I don't remember."

My attorney asked how she could not possibly remember if she had engaged in sex with someone other than her husband. She asked her if she could have possibly been drunk or been on drugs. B said that she might have had a few glasses of wine. My attorney asked her how much wine, and B said probably just a couple of glasses. She then asked her if a couple glasses of wine would have prevented her from remembering if she could have had sex outside her marriage. Once again, she said she did not remember. WOW.

My attorney then asked her if she was aware that L.S. had approached J. Golf several years before at a golf tournament and offered an apology for his affair B. She said she was not really aware of that.

My attorney asked her if she had drugs in her closet. B said that she did, but they were from years ago. My attorney asked B if she thought it was a good idea to have drugs in her closet with children in the house. B said they would not have found them. My attorney said, "I did not ask you that; I asked you if you think it is a good idea to have drugs in your closet with children in the house."

B said, "I don't see anything wrong with it."

I just kept thinking that this was getting better and better.

My attorney asked B if I was abusive. She claimed that I threw a vase at her one time. On a side note, I did throw a vase years ago at a come-to-Jesus meeting with Bubba, but it was nowhere near anyone. My attorney asked if it had hit her. She said no. My attorney asked her what she did next, and B said she started cleaning it up. My attorney asked B if she called the police or ran out the house or took all the kids to a battered woman's shelter. She said no. She also claimed that I shoved Bubba onto her bed one time. I actually do not remember that, but I did not really see that as a sign of abuse anyway. The only thing I thought that she might have brought up was the time that I was outside watering some plants and heard Bubba back-talking her mom like a spoiled brat. I dropped the hose and went inside. Bubba was lying on the couch watching TV, and I twisted her big toe and said, "Don't ever talk to your mother like that again." I was actually helping enforce some respect in our home. This was something B never did for me, ever.

My attorney then asked about The Loser. She asked B if they had sex. B proudly said, "Yes."

My attorney asked if they had unprotected sex, and she again answered yes. I am still not sure why she would answer that one, unless she thinks I had cameras installed at his rental property. I have to admit, at least she was being honest.

My attorney asked what his drink of choice was, and B told her vodka. My attorney asked B if she was aware of his multiple DWI's. She said yes, but one of them was because he had a tail light out. I still don't get that answer.

My attorney said, "He still drinks after multiple DWI's?"

B said he only drank socially.

My attorney said, "Do you think it is a good idea for him to be around the children?" and B said that he was a great guy. My attorney started asking her about many trips she had taken since I was out of the house. I know that B must have wondered how we had this information, as she did all she could to hide it from me and even threatened the kids to keep it to themselves. She would farm the kids out to friends and neighbors rather than give me the opportunity to watch them. What B did not know is that my e-mail address was the one we used when we set up her frequent flier account. I had a detailed accounting of all the trips she was taking with The Loser.

My attorney asked her about four different trips, and B acknowledged all of them. One of the trips was to Pittsburgh for The Loser's daughter's wedding. She was asked whether or not she thought that was a good idea for The Loser to take a married woman to his daughter's wedding, and B just kind of said something like "I guess so."

My attorney asked B if she ever once offered up the kids to their father while she was away. B told her no, and that I was probably playing golf or out of town myself. For this reason, we crafted a clause in the divorce decree that says I have right of first refusal to watch my kids if she ever plans to be away from them overnight. I am sure she will go by this rule.

I WAS TRAPPED IN A MISERABLE MARRIAGE AND SCREWED BY THE TERRIBLE SYSTEM!

Anyway, the deposition went great, and B must have walked out of there feeling pretty crappy about herself, unless her mental disability truly did not allow her to understand what just took place.

The next day I went to my attorney's office and gave her a bottle of wine and a thank-you card. I understood that I paid a lot of money for that deposition, but I was still very impressed with the outcome. When it was all said and done, that deposition meant nothing, as we did not go to trial. It still felt good to have her admit under oath what a lousy conniving drug-using whore she was.

MY DEPOSITION

Now it was their turn. Since we deposed B, her bottom-feeder attorney saw this as a great opportunity to run through some more marital assets and get that clock running again. I was very happy to answer any of their questions, as I had nothing to hide and had not committed the atrocities that she had. Her attorney was famous for not knowing any of the details of the case and using the deposition as a chance to become familiar with it. Rather than doing any research on all the discovery information I provided, he would rather bill us to work through the facts. Basically, the entire deposition was about money. He wanted to know where all of my money was. He did ask me who the last person I had sex with was. I told him B. He said, "You are telling me that you have not been on any dates since moving out of the house?" I said, "I'm sorry; I thought you said sex, not dates. I have had some dates, but not until more than one hundred days after being out of the house." He wanted names addresses and phone numbers. I told him that I would be glad to provide that information. He wanted to know how much money I had spent on these ladies and if I had bought them gifts or traveled with them. He then asked me if I thought B was a good mother. I proudly told him that I thought she was a terrible mother and looked right at her when I said it. He said, "Why is she so terrible?"

I went on to explain that she had drugs in her closet, she has had multiple affairs, she leaves the kids at home alone, and is more of a friend than a parent to the children, which does them no favors. He stopped me before I could go on. He asked me how I knew those were her drugs in the closet. I told him that he needs to read her deposition, as she admitted to them. He asked me how I knew that she had an affair. Once again, I reminded him to read her deposition, where she admitted to it, and to read my private investigator's report and listen to the audio tapes that I had provided in discovery. It was very clear that this bloodsucker had not gone through any of my discovery or even read the deposition we took on his client several months earlier. He then asked where the tape recordings were. We told him that they were in my discovery box at my attorney's office. He wanted those tapes right then, and my attorney would not turn them over. We explained they are available for him to listen to, but we did not have backup copies, and we

MY DEPOSITION

would not give the originals to him. We finally agreed to make copies for him. He asked me if I knew that it was illegal to wiretap a phone. I said that I did not realize it was and I don't really consider it a wiretap. I bought a voice-activated tape recorder at Radio Shack that was designed for this type of thing. He was very happy to tell me that I had broken the law in Texas. I explained that I recorded MY phone line to see what was going on in MY house with my fifteen-year-old stepdaughter when I was out of town. The place was a free-for-all once I left, and I had three of my own kids to protect. Bubba was having men over to the house for sex, and who knew what could take place? She was also setting up appointments to have tattoos and piercings. I was very proud of the fact that I was taking measures to see what was going on. Well, that was there GOTCHA moment. I admitted to recording the phone lines.

Bubba and I had a terrible relationship once she became a teenager, but she has to know how much I had done for her and her mother. This was her opportunity to get me after trying to make her go by some rules over the years. Because of the lack of discipline, she had sex with more than twenty different guys, some whose name she did not even know. I have her journal, so I have everything in writing. She was drinking, smoking pot, and taking mushrooms before she was even seventeen, and she received a DWI before she was even eighteen. She was writing letters to a guy in prison and referring to me as "the Nazi." I put up with so much but would still try to get her into church and to have her conform to some basic rules in our home. All of that meant nothing when I did not have a spouse that would support the same rules. Instead, they would party together. B just loved the fact that she was the cool mom. Bubba did not have many friends, as she had that trait like her mother, where she couldn't get along with others. Anyone who was her friend loved B and wished her own mom would be as cool as B. What seventeen-year-old would not like going to Bubba's house where you can hang out by the pool and drink beer and not even have to hide it from her mom? Sometimes I wished I had been a clerk at Walmart, where at the end of the day I would hang up my smock and come home every night. I would have been there to prevent all of this crap from going on. I am blessed to have a great job, but it does entail a lot of travel, and this was their opportunity to become PARTY CENTRAL.

MEDIATION

We had a court-mandated mediation date about one month prior to our scheduled trial date. I ended up doing it alone, without representation from my attorney. I basically had no more money to keep financing this thing and I knew what I was or was not willing to agree to in mediation. You end up paying the mediator ($1,200 from her and $1,200 from me—not a bad way to make a living) but you would also pay your attorney for all the hours that it drags on while you go back and forth with the mediator. I was just not in the mood to get billed anymore. After eight hours of mediation, we came to an agreement, and I was free to go. The mediator did pick up a catered lunch, though. By coming to this agreement, we would keep the case out of the court system, and the final decree just needed to be signed by the judge.

I probably agreed to too much, and I am sure going to feel poor when this is all over; however, I am free!

I WAS TRAPPED IN A MISERABLE MARRIAGE AND SCREWED BY THE TERRIBLE SYSTEM!

I will now have to start working to transfer all of the funds that need to go into her column of assets. Of course she had no assets in her column, which is why we needed to move so much of mine. This will be painful, but it is the way it works. I will rebuild—may take twenty years to accumulate what I am about to give her.

I have a lot of friends who have been divorced, and they say it usually just came down to "You keep your 401(k) and I will keep mine." B did not have a 401(k), a savings account, a piggy bank, or any other form of savings, so I had to finance all of this. RESENTMENT CITY!

Anyway, Hazel is very good about reminding me that money means nothing and that health, happiness, and family are what truly count. She is good for me. Even when I start to vent about B, she reminds me that I married her and that she was the mom of my children. She never jumps on the bandwagon of bashing. I really like her spirit, and I want to keep her forever. I feel like I have hit the lottery with that girl. She loves my kids too.

I was telling Hazel a story about when B hid some beef jerky from me. B's mom came in town to visit (using my frequent flier miles) and evidently she brought a huge bag of homemade deer jerky. We were all in

MEDIATION

the kitchen one day, and my son said he was hungry and wanted a snack. B told him to find something in the pantry. He asked if we still had some of that beef jerky, and both B and her mom tried to shush him. Later, my daughter told me that B's mom did in fact bring a huge bag of jerky, but they wanted to hide it from me so that I would not eat it all up. They all knew how much I loved that stuff. Hazel actually cried when she heard that story, as she could not believe they would deceive me like that over something that I cared about so much. The next day, she bought me a jerky dehydrator, and we made a huge batch that night. She was happy to see me happy, even though I popped a crown off my tooth by indulging in so much at one sitting!

My mom and sister came in town to help me decorate my condo, and they instantly fell in love with Hazel and thought she was perfect for me. My mom reminded me of the time that she flew into town and B had to pick her up at the airport, since I was still out of town. She said that B met her curbside in her SUV and was on the phone at the time. She took a split second to remove the phone from her ear and said "Hi, Ninya." All the grandkids call her Ninya. B stayed on the phone the entire time she drove my mom back to the house. My mother remembered her complaining about the women in the office to whomever she was talking to. My mom thought that was rude that B stayed on the cell phone for the entire ride, while my mother was supposed to just sit there and be quiet. My mom said she sure did not feel very welcome and believed that B was angry that she had to pick my mom up.

My mom loved to cook for us while in town, and all of the kids loved that. About the only cooking they got from B was an occasional big tray of frozen lasagna or mac and cheese. My mom loved to cook up new dished, and we all loved it. One day B was leaving for work, and my mom was making the kids breakfast before school. B told her, "If you get bored, you can dust and vacuum today." How weird can she be? I could not ever imagine saying something like that to her mom when she visited. B used people at every turn.

My mom also told me that B always hit her up for money. She never mentioned it before, as she knew how angry I would get, but B called her often to ask for donations for Bubba's stuff, such as soccer trips. My mom would mail her a check almost every single time. B's parents often mailed me a check for my birthday or Christmas, and I would mail it back to them. I told them I really appreciated all they did for the kids, but they don't need to send me money. I felt it was wrong to take cash from people when I earn about four times what they did. I really like her mom and dad and honestly believe that they know something is OFF with their daughter.

MEDIATION

I have heard that her mom and dad lived in separate parts of their home for many years, and she had to pull B's dad out of the bars almost every night. I am sure that does not make for a great family life, but they were always nice to me and to my kids. B's dad is a hard worker but reminds me of a big redneck. He was not happy about wearing a tie at our wedding, and the very second the ceremony was over, he ripped that tie off and started boozing.

B has two brothers, and I really like them and their wives too. They are both divorced now as well. I guess some things run in a family. It's got to be sad for their parents to know that all three kids have had marriage failures and B's had two. I am sure there are more to come. That may be why her dad starts drinking red wine as soon as he gets up each morning. He buys the big jugs of cheap red wine and drinks from a plastic cup...ALL DAY.

We went to court on October 30, as B and her attorney filed a motion to force me to sign the divorce decree, even though I did not agree with some wording her attorney sneaked into it. I felt like it would finally be a good day for me in court, because how can they make me sign something that did not line up with our mediated settlement agreement? I did not think there was a chance in hell that I could lose this argument, as it was all in black and white. Well, it was like Part II of *Candid Camera*, and I lost again. I can't believe everything kept going against me. The judge was very arrogant and rude, and he generally takes the side of the woman, who in many cases probably is a helpless victim. He never gave me a chance to explain anything and told me that he did not know the circumstances of our case. That is when I told him, "I know. I want to tell you the circumstances," and he did not let me finish. He said that we agreed to go to mediation rather than have a trial, and he would not hear anything. I told him that I would have loved to go to trial so I could have displayed all of her affairs, drugs in the closet, lying about car payment amounts and income, etc., but I ran out of money. I spent more than $163,000 in attorney fees, and it raped me of ALL our savings. He rolled his eyes and did not feel the least bit sorry for a guy that was punished by the system. He ruled in her favor for the bill that I did not agree to pay while the house was still on the market; however, I was used to getting screwed every single time, even though I thought I had a clear winner on this one. The judges just don't give a damn about you or any of the background or history. He was an elected judge who has been there forever and probably hated his job and the people he had to serve.

Our system really sucks. He signed the decree and it was officially over. I am still on the hook for 25% of the house payment, insurance, taxes, and HELOC loan until the house sells, but at least it is better than paying 100% that I did for a year and a half under temporary orders. I gave myself a raise that day and may actually be able to pay all my bills out of my monthly paycheck, rather than continue to sell stock and borrow money. I still owe my attorneys about $3,500, but I will not be in any hurry to pay that bill off. I may mail them $20.00 per month just to keep them from suing me. They did NOTHING for me. Nothing at all. I should have represented myself from day one. There is so much truth in the fact that the attorneys drain all of your money until it is gone, and then they walk away. I really wonder if our divorce would have been over a long time ago, had I only had $30,000 in savings. How could Tom Cruise and Katie Holmes be divorced faster than me? I am sure it was because at least one of them was smart enough to come to some form of agreement to get it behind them. I always thought Tom Cruise was a little strange, but B is much stranger. She milked the system and took advantage of the temporary orders that gave her no incentive to get the divorce finalized.

I know it is too soon to start talking about marriage again, but I really love Hazel. I now know that she is the one and there will never be any reason to look for someone else. The other day, she even told me that if we were ever to get engaged, she would not even want a diamond for a ring. She really does not like jewelry that much and would just prefer a small silver band. Is this a dream? B would constantly beg and beg for more diamonds. I gave her an almost two-carat diamond ring, and it was only about four years later that she was hinting that we should upgrade it to a bigger stone. I said "WHAT? I would hope that the stone I gave you would have some sentimental value, never mind the fact that it is bigger than all of her friends' diamonds and bigger than probably ninety-nine percent of the world's population would ever receive." Nonetheless, she always talked about having that stone made into a pendant, and she would like to receive a new stone for her wedding band, something closer to four carats. I later found out that a four-carat ring is not double the price of a two-carat ring. It does not work that way. The larger you go, the price goes up dramatically. A four-carat ring could be close to $100,000. That fact did not matter to her, as she had no concern if I had the money or not. She would recommend financing it, if necessary.

I gave her diamond ear studs, half carats each. She liked them, even though I could instantly tell she wished they had been bigger. She lost one of them at an amusement park in California, and you would think the world was coming to an end. I think she worshiped diamonds more than she worshiped our Lord and Savior. Anyway, I ended up getting sucked into buying her two new one-caret (each ear) diamonds.

She used the other half-carat stone to stick into a ring that was already full of diamonds that she inherited from her grandmother and the stone she had from her first marriage. She loved growing her diamond collection.

B sent me an e-mail the other day and told me to be sure to have our son at his counseling session Saturday at 4:00. I responded, "What are you talking about? I did not know anything about a counseling session, and why does he need it?"

We are supposed to consult each other before signing the kids up for something like this. She told me that he made a comment about if he died, I would just go to the golf course rather than the funeral. I am sure he was joking, but it probably stems from the years of her trying to convince the kids that golf was more important to me than the kids. All three kids had a counseling session that day, and the middle daughter later told me that my oldest daughter cried and told him that she loves me very much, even though she is not that close to me right now. They all three agreed that their mom was trying to put bad things in their mind about me and was even trying to keep them from seeing me. I am sure she will fire that counselor if she gets a report back from him that she will not be winning Mom of the Year anytime soon.

I WAS TRAPPED IN A MISERABLE MARRIAGE AND SCREWED BY THE TERRIBLE SYSTEM!

I really feel bad for the kids, and I cannot imagine growing up with a whack-job mom like her. My mom was one of my best role models. If I did not travel for a living, I would fight hard for custody, even though it is a very difficult process. I just hope they will chose to come live with me someday when they finally learn it is time to remove themselves from that psycho environment. I would welcome them to be with me anytime and know they will grow up better as a result.

Both of the younger ones have developed their mom's bad habit of saying "Oh my god," and I constantly remind them to say "gosh" instead. I just pray that they can have normal loving relationships someday after being around a bipolar screamer nut job for so many years. I really don't think Bubba will ever get married, and if she does, that marriage will be doomed. She is a huge product of her mother, and for that fact I am sad. Even though she is suing me, I am sad for her. That subject may be my next book, *The stepdaughter that I helped raise for nineteen years is suing me for wire taping her phone conversations nine years ago.* Can it get any better than this? I know this all sounds like fiction, but it is true. Just when I thought I had my legal troubles behind me from the divorce, I get served in my own driveway for a lawsuit that the stepdaughter, Bubba, has filed. I can't image who may be behind this motive. In Texas it is illegal to record your own phone lines. This is a civil lawsuit, not criminal, and there can be a $10,000 award of damages for each occurrence. This is B and Bubba's attempt to extort even more money out of me, and they certainly found a different blood-sucking attorney to take on this case. I guess ambulance chasing must be off-season right now. There is a four-year statute of limitations, so I'm not sure how far they will get with this lawsuit, but I still had to hire an attorney to represent me and burn through more cash that I don't have.

Bubba is about to graduate from law school, so this lawsuit may be some sort of project for her. I can't imagine that she really suffered any damages by my recording our phones when she was not even supposed to be using the phone, because she was being punished for doing drugs, having sex at sixteen, and drinking under age. Nothing surprises me nowadays, so we shall see what becomes of this lawsuit. I just wonder what B and her mother will try to sue me for when this one is over.

I am trying to complete this book and more things keep going on that I must write about. The divorce was final as of October 30, and I feel like I have been reamed out with no lube, even though I am happy to have it over with. Now B has hired a new attorney to see if he can do better than what we agreed to in mediation. She believes everything was slanted toward me and that she should not have to give me 25% of our home equity when the house sells. I think B and The Loser are trying to buy the house, but they cannot obtain financing. She does not have enough income, and he probably has lousy credit. They are in panic mode. They have been canceling showings of the home, and they even took the sign out of the front yard and leaned it against the house. If I were driving by, I would think it meant the house had sold.

I now have the ability to ask for a court-appointed receiver to be responsible for selling the home, and the receiver can get the sale done very quickly. The receiver basically starts lowering the price until the house sells. I am all for this, even though it will cost me as well. I have gone through so much cash in the past year and half, who cares at this point? I just want the house sold so that I am no longer on the hook for the monthly bills. B offered to let me keep my North Carolina land and a portion of an IRA. Both of these are going to be transferred to her as part of our mediated agreement, but she would rather let me keep those if I can give her my 25% of the house. I am actually in favor of doing this, but I told her attorney that she needs to have Bubba drop the lawsuit against me, so that I can be finished with feeding attorneys more money. She blasted me with an e-mail the other day and said that I am the one who always has to change things, and she is going to tell the kids that I am trying to kick them out of the house. I reminded her that we were now divorced and everything had been agreed on. I was willing to work with her on letting her keep the house, but FOR ONCE, something had to go my way. Not only would she have to get that lawsuit dropped, but she would also have to obtain a mortgage, so that my name is no longer associated with the loan. She may finally feel trapped herself. I told her attorney I would give them one week to make a decision; otherwise I was going to move forward with filing a motion to appoint a receiver. We shall see. She does not like the fact that I, for once, have a little power over something.

I received an e-mail the other day from my middle daughter, the daughter who has always been my biggest fan. She said that she was disappointed in me for not working with her mom to keep them in the house. She said that they all want to stay there and that the house is very important to them. I told her that we will need to talk, as she is getting some bad information. I took both girls to church on Sunday, and then we went to lunch afterwards. There we had our big revelation meeting. I told them EVERYTHING. I made it very clear that I was not trying to win points or turn them against their mother. I even told them that they are still required to honor their mother, but it was time they learn some facts about things that have taken place over the years. If B is going to use the children to try to manipulate me, I will let them in on things I had never brought up before.

I find it very sad that they now know their mom is a total whack job. They always joked that she was crazy, but now they have some real muscle behind it. I explained that we will never have to talk about the subject again, but I wanted them to know what I had put up with for the latter years of our marriage. They both cried when they learned about the affairs, and they felt sorry for me. Later that night, I received an e-mail from my middle daughter, and she said that I was the best dad in the world and she loved me very much.

I had mixed emotions in the meeting, but the girls needed to know the truth about their mom rather than the lies she was feeding them about me. I chose not to tell my son, as he is still too young. I explained to my daughters that everything I told them was 100% true and that I had proof to back up all my facts. I also told them to ask their mom to prove something when she told them a lie about me.

I also just found out that while I was out of town on a business trip, the kids came over to have dinner with Hazel. The subject of affairs came up, and my son told everyone about a time when he was probably five or six that he woke up late and came into the kitchen

MEDIATION

where there were three men standing around in their underwear. One of the men ducked behind the counter to act like he was not there. B was standing there with them and acted very surprised that he woke up and came into the room.

I was sure played as a fool. It was sad to me that my son had this memory on his mind all these years. He had never even told me about it, and he probably does not want to hurt me. As much as I would love to reveal to him about all the others, I don't.

ADVICE SECTION

I wanted to spend a few minutes going over some things that I believe can be helpful to anyone who may feel TRAPPED as I was. I am certainly not a lawyer and give this advice only as an average guy who has been severely screwed by the system and by lawyers that are concerned only with running the clock on clients. First of all, if you are trapped in your marriage, please figure out a way to start hiding some cash so that you at least have a pot to piss in when you get removed from your house during the temporary orders. I am not going to say if or how much I had socked away, I would sure recommend having a nice little slush fund. You can hide cash by doing a little at a time, and you will be very glad to have that little nest egg if you get filed on when you least expect it. It is sad to be in a marriage where you feel the need to take this action, but trust me, WATCH YOUR BACK. If you live with someone like I did, counseling and church will not make any difference in getting your marriage back on track.

ADVICE SECTION

Don't waste money hiring a private detective to prove that your wife is having an affair. Even though I feel good about catching her, it really means nothing. In Texas, at least, there is no big change in the distribution of assets after adultery. I have heard that Tennessee and other states do consider adultery a crime against the marriage and there can be huge swings in the outcome. Once again, my luck is to live in Texas, where you can basically be having sex on the judge's desk and it does not make a difference.

Make sure you know the laws of your state when it comes to recording your phone lines. I was proud to admit that I had recordings of my wife being unfaithful in our marriage, but it cost me another lawsuit.

When you are asked to move out under temporary orders, get as much stuff out of the house as you possibly can. I figured that I would just get my items later, as the judge would surely split the property in half. Well, this equal distribution can be very hard to achieve. When I moved out, all I took was my office furniture, my clothes, very few personal items, and a Bose radio (something to listen to while in my office). You would think I cleaned out Fort Knox. She must have brought up that Bose radio twenty times since I moved out and how badly she needed it back. She had twelve TVs, two other radios, and a surround sound intercom system in the home, but those things did not matter. She was furious that I got out of the house with the Bose. We had 5,500 square feet of very expensive furniture, furniture that I bought. She did not want me to have any of it. I was able to negotiate a few items so that I could start my life over again. Get anything you want when you leave the first time, as it can sure be a cat fight to obtain anything later.

Don't be eager to settle at the temporary hearing. I agreed to a bunch of crap rather than seeing the judge, as I thought the process would be over in a couple of months. If I had it to do over again, I would prefer to see the judge if I did not get everything that I wanted. I was actually willing to be fair at the temporary hearing, but then ended up getting my head handed to me. I am not so sure the judge would have even made me move out. There was a chance that B would have been asked to leave, since she was having the affair. I will never know.

If I had to do everything over again, I would not even hire an attorney. I made many offers to my wife to get the divorce settled, and she just went dumb on me. If I had not had an attorney, her attorney would have been forced to deal directly with me. Our divorce should have been settled in two or three months, and B certainly did not end up doing any better by dragging it out for sixteen months, other than living in a free house for all that time and enjoying the

ADVICE SECTION

temporary orders. She would have had much more money to split, had we settled in the beginning. Those lawyers could have purchased four new Cadillacs for what I paid them. If I represented myself, her attorney would have had to request all the discovery directly from me. Why did I pay a law firm to manage all that paperwork time and time again? I could have done it myself. You are always allowed to represent yourself. If she still did not want to settle, I would have just met her at the mediation, which was court mandated anyway. The mediation is where we ended up settling after more than fifteen months and $163,000 in attorney fees.

I honestly cannot think of one thing my attorney did for me. The deposition of B was great and my attorney made her look like an idiot; however, none of that mattered. If you are not aware of how to file motions and ask for court dates, you can always hire a lawyer or paralegal to perform these tasks, and just be sure they know you are representing yourself. If I could go back in time, this is what I would have done. Once the process starts, stay close to the kids and your friends. Go to church and work out. You need to stay busy and keep your stress to a minimum. God is great, and you can lean on him during the process. I realize I used some bad words in my book, but I am a true believer. I am convinced that what goes around comes around. I have never prayed that anything bad would happen to B, but I just feel it in my gut that her day is coming—not necessarily death or being harmed, but just something is going to hit her, and she will realize this is her payback for dragging me through the mud when I was the good guy. She loved the fact that the system worked in her favor and she got away with lie after lie. I don't even have to be around to witness "her day," but I sure feel it is coming. She drained my savings accounts by dragging out the divorce process as long as she possibly could. She did not give a damn about that money, as anything she got in the divorce was better than what she had before. She will never know how hard it was and how disciplined you must be to save the kind of money that I paid to finance this divorce and award her all her newfound wealth. It would be easy for me to say "May she rot in hell," but I am not going to. God forgives all, and she can find favor with him and her children and even me, if she makes some adjustments in her life.

My friend Randy has written a book and keeps telling me that I need at least 40,000 words to publish a book. I told him that I am not interested in putting dead weight into my book or trying to stretch it out by writing a bunch of stuff that is not interesting to the reader. I am not expecting this book to be a national bestseller, but it is certainly good therapy for me, and I want others to know what can happen to a guy when a woman goes wild and decides to break up a family and make some changes in her life.

ADVICE SECTION

Just when I think I am about to wind down my writings, more stuff comes to me. For that reason, I am going to wait and see what happens before I get too eager to complete it. The Bubba (wiretapping) lawsuit has really heated up. We were planning to depose her on January 9, but she did not send in her interrogatory answers that were due. My attorney sent her attorney a list of questions to answer that he needed before holding a deposition. She was three weeks late in returning them, so her lack of response made us think she was dropping the lawsuit. He sent her attorney a notice stating that we were canceling the deposition until we had her answers returned. A few days later the attorney forwarded Bubba's answers and made a demand for payment of $275,000. What a joke! She wanted $275,000 because I recorded the phone lines more than eight years ago, while she was going wild in my house and did not have a mother who would do anything about it. Her damages consisted of mental anguish, punitive damages, and attorney fees. So much for this thing going away.

My attorney said we could make her an offer to see if she would settle. I told him NO WAY. The issue comes down to principles, and I am not going to give her a dime; however, I will have to continue feeding my attorney money to keep representing me. This instance is just another example of how helpless you can be if someone decides he or she really wants to screw with you.

I WAS TRAPPED IN A MISERABLE MARRIAGE AND SCREWED BY THE TERRIBLE SYSTEM!

While this lawsuit is going on, I am still trying to work with B to have our wording corrected in the divorce decree, since she suddenly decided she wants to keep the house. She could never keep that house if she had not sunk her claws into some other fellow, The Loser, to help her maintain the materialistic lifestyle she so desperately needs. From what the real estate agents have told me, he has cash flow and income but must have terrible credit, because they have not been able to obtain a new mortgage to buy me out. With our new agreement, I will keep more of my retirement account (money that I was supposed to award her) and my North Carolina land in exchange for my percentage of the home equity she would owe me when the house sold. I agreed to make this change to our divorce decree, as it would be better financially for me; however, I want my name off the mortgage, to make sure she does not mess up my credit. I think we have finally settled on a condition that will give her 365 days to obtain a new mortgage, and if she misses a payment or pays late, it will void our arrangement, and I will still be entitled to receive my portion of the equity.

I have been warned by many friends not to trust that she will make the payment. It will be up to me to call each month to make sure the payment is getting sent in. As long as The Loser does not dump her, we should be OK. I figure he will move in soon, as he is currently a renter nearby but spends most of his time at the house. The kids do not want him moving in, or so they have told me.

I recently found out that B has been out of town over a weekend TWICE in the past four weeks. She failed to notify me, which is a direct violation of the divorce decree. I have right of first refusal, which means she MUST contact me if she is planning to go out of town (overnight) without the kids. She MUST give me the option to watch my kids while she is away. She has failed to do this twice since the divorce has been final, maybe more. I found out that one weekend the kids all stayed over at The Loser's house. One of my oldest daughter's friends was part of the party, and she is a known pot smoker. I sent an e-mail to B and told her that I want our kids drug tested. No response. I did get an e-mail a few days later from my oldest, and she basically told me that we should not waste our money on a drug test, since her mom and I don't really have extra money right now. I told her, "Don't worry; I can afford it." I received another e-mail where she then flat out admitted to using pot and said she did not believe it was that big of a deal and that she needs to put our relationship on hold for now, since I am trying to control every aspect of her life. WHAT? I think that must have been B typing, as it sounded just like her. I told her that I was very disappointed that she felt like there was something wrong with a dad that would have a problem with his seventeen-year-old daughter doing illegal drugs. I have not heard from her since. I guess she wants to put our relationship on hold. Should I drug test her or not? I hate always being the bad guy, but someone needs to get control of what is going on over there. It just makes me sad that the parent who does not have primary custody really seems to have no power.

A week or two went by, and I did not hear from the girls. I did have my son stay with me on my weekends, and he seems to enjoy being with me. I noticed that my oldest daughter gave me a Like to a recent Facebook post from when Hazel and I were out to dinner somewhere. I was glad she made the first move to contact me. I sent her a message and told her that I loved her and missed her. She said, "Are you sure you still like me?" I told her that I love her no matter what.

I met the girls for dinner one night and nothing was brought up about pot or drug testing. I just wanted to see them, and I really do love them so much. I am just going to continue to be a good role model for them, even though I don't get to see them much.

B sent me some stuff by certified mail. She loves to use certified mail, so she can prove she mailed something. I just wish she would either hand it to me when I pick up the kids or mail it regular mail. I don't always have time to go to the post office and wait in line to retrieve and sign for certified mail. This time I kept ignoring the notices and never picked up the mail. It was eventually returned to her, which had to have steamed her, as she wasted the extra postage to send it certified. She sent it along with my son, and it consisted of a prescription for him in the amount of $15.00, a copy of her payment to the orthodontist for $310.00, and passport applications for the kids that I needed to sign me and get notarized. I have all of these papers sitting on my desk, and I am just not in a big hurry to accommodate B these days. She sent me an e-mail and said she needed the checks for reimbursement and the completed passport forms when I come to pick up my son Thursday. I just ignored her. I believe she, The Loser, and the kids want to go to the Bahamas for spring break, but I am just not so sure I want my kids going out of the country with her and The Loser, especially since I have no idea what the guy does for a living. I have heard that he is in the Bahamas as well as Southern Florida much of the time. It makes me wonder if he is some form of drug dealer. I hate to be a total control freak, but I am truly concerned about this issue. There are plenty of things that happen in foreign countries that you can't control, and you don't have the good old US government there to turn to for help. Remember the Natalie Holloway event?

I WAS TRAPPED IN A MISERABLE MARRIAGE AND SCREWED BY THE TERRIBLE SYSTEM!

When I was picking up my son the other night, B came walking up to the car. WOW, I can't even make eye contact with her, because of all my resentment. She looks TERRIBLE. She has aged something awful and is getting wrinkled from all those years of worshiping the sun. Anyway, she came right up to the car and wanted to know if I had her checks. I promised I would not shaft her on the $7.50 that I owe her for some medicine, but that I don't like writing checks for such a small amount. I asked her if she could just please hold onto those types of things, and once she had several months' worth, I would then pay her. She asked me about the orthodontics bill. I told her I paid the orthodontist directly and actually paid him off in total for my share, which was about $700, after asking them for a printout on the account, so I could verify I was not getting screwed or lied to. She then asked about the passports, and I told her that I would try to get to them when possible.

I think she is trying to get the passports rushed through as quickly as possible, since spring break is around the corner and the Bahamas trip cannot happen without them. She honestly said, "Can you please get those done right away? I don't ask for much."

I thought I was at a Ron White stand-up comedy show. She does not ask for much? This is the hag that dragged the divorce on for a year and half so she could enjoy all the temporary orders. She also wanted as absolute much money and possessions as she could get her grubby hands on. She even wanted half of my Rolex watch. Was I supposed to cut it in half? The lady is very greedy, but because of her mental illness, she honestly does not think she asks for much.

I am in no hurry to sign for those passports. Let her take me to court, and we will see if the judge makes me sign them. I have plenty of information I would like to give him as to why I don't want my younger two kids going out of the country. Maybe I can also take that opportunity to tell him that she is not living up to her decree agreement on the right of first refusal. In addition, I understand that she fired her third attorney, so I am not sure if she is planning to hire another one.

I have been dating Hazel for more than four months now, and she is so great. I am truly in love and did not think it could happen this fast, if even at all. She is the most supporting, kind person I have ever met, and I honestly do not believe she would have it in her to be unfaithful. I will marry that woman. She has recently had the opportunity to experience B. My company car has a Bluetooth speaker-phone system, so all calls go through my radio. I have never learned how to take it off that setting, in case I want to keep things private, so Hazel has witnessed B calling me on several occasions to demand money, belittle me, etc. Hazel said that B acts like a rabid dog and appears to be the type of person that may be on a controlled substance. One night B went from topic to topic with me, and I continued to smoke her on every issue. I could tell she was very frustrated. Hazel said that I was too nice to her and needed to stand up more and give it right back to her. It does not matter how I talk to her, as she is so darned bipolar that the fuzz in her mind blocks out everything I try to tell her. She kept telling me to stop putting things in the kids' minds that are not true. I asked her time and time again for an example, as I HAVE NEVER LIED to the kids. She could not offer an example.

We found out that B has been creeping my Facebook page. She sent me some e-mails that basically were word for word as I had posted. I think B is using the kids' accounts to see my posts, as I am sure not a friend of hers. Hazel posted, "Wow, Facebook creeping does not surprise me. Hi, B, let's have coffee sometime."

My sister chimed in and said, "Why don't you guys just block that crazy LOON so that she can't creep you anymore?"

Well, these comments started a mini-war. My daughters started posting to my sister that she should not call their mom a LOON. My sister told them that she is

ADVICE SECTION

much more than a LOON, but she was trying to keep it clean. They called my sister a bitch; B called her a fat-ass back stabber; and they all went back and forth a few times.

I instantly took my Facebook account down, as I have always prided myself in keeping it professional and Christ-like. It was obvious that B was snooping around, and it bugs the heck out of her that I am happy with Hazel. I have never once tried to look on her account, and I could not care less. If she is happy with The Loser, so be it. Maybe they will get married soon; it will be his fourth wife.

B told me in one e-mail that all his ex-wives were the problem. If that is true, he has no idea what he is getting into. I really should sit down for a beer with the guy and enlighten him, but no one did it for me, so he will just learn on his own eventually.

The Bubba lawsuit is still alive and well. It is the drama she and her mother now need, since the divorce is final. Everyone I talk to about it cannot believe that this can happen. First of all, most people cannot believe it is illegal to record your own phone line at your own house. My attorney was not even aware of that statute until he did some research. He said there is not much case law on it, since no one ever sues for it. It's my luck that I am dealing with B and Bubba, who are SUE HAPPY. They are latching onto the fact that I admitted in my deposition that I recorded the phone lines. Evidently there is no defense for doing it. I can't believe there can't be a defense. I would surely murder someone who was about to murder my children, so there has to be a defense to anything you do. Just like speeding, you get a chance to tell the judge why you were speeding. It may not get you off the hook, but you have the opportunity to explain your actions. I proudly admitted to recording my phone lines, as I did not know it was illegal, and I was trying to learn what was going on in my house while I was away. Bubba was only fifteen years old and already having sex. She was doing drugs and drinking and writing to a prisoner. She was having strange guys come over to the house while I was out of town. All of this was occurring when I had three young children. My attorney said he can truly understand why I would do it and so would almost any jury; however, we may not even get an opportunity to go down that road, since WHY does not matter or mean anything. I still need to pinch myself to make sure this is really happening. About the worst law I have ever broken is going fourteen miles over the speed limit, or one time I got caught for doing the California stop at a stop sign. I have a pilot friend that told me he knows of many coworkers that regularly record their wives while out of town. I told him he had better warn them about the wiretapping laws. It does not matter that my wife was having

ADVICE SECTION

extramarital affairs and the kid was having sex parties while I was on business trips, but it sure is a horrific crime that I was trying to find out about it. It does not seem like common sense to me.

My attorney received a demand letter from Bubba's attorney asking for $250,000 to settle the case. There were nine recordings of her conversations at $10,000 each plus mental anguish charges, punitive damage charges, and estimated attorney fees, which is how they came up with that total. We did not respond. Later we got another letter stating that they would be glad to settle for $95,000. I guess her mental anguish was not as bad as she originally thought.

First of all, I don't have any money left after the divorce, so they are clearly trying to break me financially. He asked me how to respond to their demand. I said that I would like to tell them to shove it up their asses, but perhaps we needed to be a bit more diplomatic. He will respond by informing them that we plan to defend the lawsuit to the full extent. We are now going to schedule a deposition on Bubba. I can't wait to sit across the table from her while we ask her all kinds of questions about her past behavior.

B and I went back and forth on some e-mails the other day. She was hitting me up for $7.50 (one half of the amount I owe her for a reimbursement on a prescription). I told her please to hold these small bills, and when they add up to $100 or more, I would pay her. I don't like writing checks for $7.50, and I could never trust her if I handed her cash. She wanted to show her teeth and told me that I had to reimburse her within so many days when she presents me a bill, with no flexibility at all. Everything has to be by the book when it's to her benefit, but heaven forbid she go by the rules when it could impact her. I think she became frustrated with me when I refused to reimburse her for one of my daughters' lost orthodontics retainer. I think it was the third time she had lost it, and they cost about $250.00 to replace. The orthodontist's office actually sent me an e-mail stating the B paid half, and the office wanted to make sure I was going to pay the other half so that B could pick the appliance up that evening. I was not at all eager to help her out on that one. I responded to the e-mail by explaining that it was not a medical bill and that she could take it out of the very healthy child support check I provide her each month. The woman was very nice and said she totally understood.

B also presented me with a bill for counseling for the kids. The counselor mailed me the statement for $150.00, and I simply forwarded it to B. I also do not consider this expense medical, and if the kids truly needed counseling, it would be something we would need to discuss and it would need to be an in-network

ADVICE SECTION

provider, in order for me to participate with shared cost. I enclosed a note explaining that the kids do not need counseling (they have all told me this themselves) and that they need a mother that will stay in town a little more often and one that does not try to prevent them from spending time with their father. All the kids have told me that they end up bashing their mom in the counseling sessions, and she truly does try to keep them from me, even though she would never admit it.

My response must have struck a nerve with B, so she blocked all the kids' phones from me again. I cannot call my kids on their cell phones, and they cannot call me. I am sure a judge would not like this action, but do I really want to take her to court and burn more dollars and time? I sent her another e-mail explaining that blocking me from contact with my kids was ridiculous and that I would never dream of doing the same to her, no matter what she might do to agitate me. She will always be their mom, and I honestly would not try to prevent the children from seeing or calling her. WOW! She sent me a note back and told me that she pays for their cell phones and that no one is going to tell her what she can do with her phones. She suggested that I purchase some cell phones for all of them, if I want to have contact with them. Boy, I must be stupid. That would make sense for the kids to carry around TWO cell phones. Why didn't I think of that? Has anyone out there ever heard of such a thing? I PROMISE I am not making any of this up just to add drama to my book.

I have not added to my book in several weeks, but I am now on a trip from Los Angeles, California, back to Texas and couldn't get my computer fired up fast enough. I had a Facebook message from my middle daughter (fifteen years old). Remember, she can't call me, so contact through the computer is our only way of communicating, unless she calls me from one of her friends' phones. The Facebook message stated that she and her older sister are tired of their school and want to try a new school in Florida and that they all want to move to Florida for a new start and that she hopes I will not try to control them and keep them in Texas. She told me that they will just give it a try for one year, and if they don't like it, they will come back. She told me that they don't see me much anyway, so I should be OK with it.

I responded that I hope she was just joking, as I could never imagine them moving 1,500 miles away. Evidently The Loser has some marketing job in the Bahamas, which is probably why they made so many trips to Fort Lauderdale. I also offered up that they could come live with me, and we could all move to California. I told them California is much better than Florida anyway. I told her we could talk about

ADVICE SECTION

it tomorrow night, and she said that she couldn't see me tomorrow, as she is busy. She is starting to act like her mom, if she does not get her way. I am not even sure what to do next. I do have domicile protection in the divorce decree that limits B and the kids to moving only within a two-county area. I am sure she will want to negotiate something so that they can all go start their new life in Florida. I will volunteer to let them stay with me, and she will not even have to pay me child support. She may even offer to let me off the hook for the tremendous amount of child support I am paying, but child support is not the issue for me. I would rather see my kids. My son just turned thirteen, and I believe I would see them, at best, only two or three times per year if they moved. That schedule will not work for me. I may actually have some power for a change, even though they all may hate me for exercising it. I am sure B is preaching that life will be just like Disneyland if they all move to Florida, and now I will be the bad guy if I make them stay. This is truly a no-win situation. Kids don't see the bigger picture, and I wished they loved me so much that they could not imagine moving away from me. Their frontal lobe has not fully developed at their age, so they cannot correctly reason right from wrong. B's frontal lobe never developed either and may have been stunted from marijuana or Prozac use; I'm not sure. I cannot believe she is honestly putting them up to begging me to bless their move.

◄ I WAS TRAPPED IN A MISERABLE MARRIAGE AND SCREWED BY THE TERRIBLE SYSTEM!

I just found out about this potential move a few hours ago, so I am pounding these computer keys pretty firmly. I think I may need counseling now to see what direction I need to take. Maybe this entire thing is a test, a test from either God or B to see how far I can be pushed. I wonder if she will be willing to let them live with me so that she can move. We will see. It's pretty obvious that she has not made the kids a priority since she met The Loser. If she tries to sue me for slander, I have plenty of witnesses who will agree with my statement.

My mom is coming into town tonight. Her flight lands about thirty minutes after mine, and Hazel will be picking us up. We will have a lot to talk about tonight and what direction to take from here. I will update again soon. In addition, the deposition on the Bubba lawsuit is scheduled for next month, so we continue to move forward with that one. I am ready to get lawyers off the payroll.

My mom was in town for a full week and we had a great visit. I had my son for about four days of the visit, and he had a blast spending time with my mom. My two daughters made no effort to come see their grandmother, which made me very angry, as she is a wonderful woman who has done nothing but good things for her grandkids. I told them I was very embarrassed and disappointed that they did not make any attempt to visit, especially since they only live five miles away and have plenty of free time on their hands. I told them, "Do you know what I would give to be able to spend some time with my grandparents if they were still alive?" Nothing fazes them as long as they are having fun for the moment. I am sad that they are being brainwashed by their mom, and who knows what she may have told them? I think I may need another COME-TO-JESUS meeting with them.

My mom told me that she wants to take me to Africa this summer for a two-week trip. One week would be doing mission work and the second week would be a safari. She did this same trip about five years ago and said it was the best trip she ever took. She wants to treat me to this vacation after all that I have been through. I think I will start saving my vacation time and take her up on this offer.

The deposition of Bubba just took place, as did mine. Her attorney appears to be a real ambulance chaser. We deposed Bubba for about 1.5 hours, and her attorney had only about twenty minutes of questions for me. B came with Bubba to the deposition, but we would not let her in the room. She had to stay in the lobby. It is amazing that she drove Bubba to the deposition after telling me that she had nothing to do with the lawsuit. I assure you that she is the mastermind behind this, especially since she is addicted to attorneys.

Bubba pretty much admitted to having sex, doing drugs, drinking, writing to prisoners, and meeting older guys online, and she also believed that there was no reason for me to be concerned as the head of the house. WOW! I actually felt sorry for her.

It is hard to feel sorry for someone who is suing me and has caused me to spend close to $10,000 so far just to defend myself from this ridiculous lawsuit. Even if I win, I will not win, as I am spending money each month, and she found some ambulance chaser to take this on a contingency. At one time, she was asking for almost $300,000. She had pain and suffering and punitive damages and attorney fees all rolled into it. Now it looks like they are just seeking the $10,000 per recording of her voice, and it appears that there are nine of them. On one of the calls, someone asked for me and she called me to the phone. I guess that is really worth $10,000 of damages. Several of the calls were her contacting a guy named Pig who does tattoos and piercings. She was fifteen at the time.

My attorney asked her if she believed there was any reason for ME to be concerned as a parent with the fact that she was bringing strangers into the house, having sex, doing drugs, drinking, writing letters to a prisoner, and obtaining piercings and tattoos at fifteen, especially when I had three younger children in the house and I was traveling. She honestly said "No."

He then asked her why she believed there was no reason for me to be concerned, and she said because she did not do it all the time.

Her attorney asked me if I was a police officer or switchboard operator and had authority to record the phone lines. He also wanted to know how I obtained the device and how I hooked it up. I admitted that I was not a police officer or switch board operator, but I was the head of my house, and it was my house and my phone lines, and I did not know what else to do, since I was very concerned with the safety of my family members, including her. I also explained that it was a simple tape recorder that I bought at Radio Shack and plugged into an outlet in the garage. It was not some grand wiretapping plot like Watergate. In addition, I was not trying to obtain trade secrets from a competitor or blackmail anyone. I was flat out trying to find out why all this crap was going on in my house while I was out of town, and I had a wife who was on Prozac at the time and did not seem to give a damn about any of this activity. Anyway, I felt good after leaving the deposition, but I also felt that way after leaving the deposition for the divorce, and it did not get me far. I keep thinking that my day is coming.

I WAS TRAPPED IN A MISERABLE MARRIAGE AND SCREWED BY THE TERRIBLE SYSTEM!

Hazel is supportive, and she just can't believe what they are trying to do to keep extorting money from me. They just won't let go. B had the affair and wanted out of the marriage. She evidently hates me, even though I am a very good father to our children. It just makes you wonder why she can't go away peacefully and leave me alone. She has absolutely no shame for her actions and multiple affairs, but to top it off, she wants to keep dragging me through the mud.

I sent B an e-mail the other day to let her know I would be picking up my son after school on Thursday, which is my day, and also asked if he had any activities over the weekend that I needed to know about. I think I struck a nerve, as she probably was not aware that I had back-to-back weekends with him, because of the way the month worked out in regard to my visitation. She blasted an e-mail back stating that I was a loser and that she finally met a real man and is very happy and that she was surprised I even wanted to spend time with my kids and that it is no wonder my daughters don't want to have a relationship with me.

I should have just let it go. My sister keeps telling me to ignore those types of e-mails from B, as she just loves confrontation and I should not add fuel to the fire. Sorry, but I could not resist. I blasted an e-mail right back and told her that I was glad she is happy and that she continues to keep telling me that fact. I also explained that I am sorry she thinks I am a loser, and I guess she also thought her first husband was a loser and then named about five guys (other guys she had affairs with) and told her they must have all been losers too. However, I am glad she finally met a GREAT guy and that she should marry him so that he can have his fourth wife. I also told her that most women who have multiple affairs on their husbands and then want out usually quietly go away.

She is like a slimy booger that you cannot get off your damn finger. She just continues to cause problems and has absolutely no shame for her actions. I told her to ask my daughters directly if they do not want to have a relationship with me, as I know it is not true. Her only response to my e-mail was that she believed I was truly sick and ill. HA HA.

I saw my fifteen-year-old and told her that her mom said I was a loser and that the girls did not want to have a relationship with me. I said that I did not believe it to be true. It made her so angry and she said she would have a talk with her mom about that comment. She told me that she could not be prouder to have me as a father and would not trade me for anything. I just love it when a fifteen-year-old will stand up to her mom's lies.

I WAS TRAPPED IN A MISERABLE MARRIAGE AND SCREWED BY THE TERRIBLE SYSTEM!

Evidently she confronted her mom about those comments, and B just started stuttering and really had nothing to say about it. My daughter also told me that The Loser moved into the house. I knew that would eventually happen. He was able to give up his rental property and move into my house. I don't really know who is using who, but I figure it will all blow up someday when they realize their entire relationship is built on lies and deceit. I just hope the kids are OK. My daughter said it is rather uncomfortable having him there.

Hazel and I had dinner with Dave and his wife, the friends I lived with for one year while going through the divorce. They really like Hazel, and we try to get together once in a while, even though it is tough, because Dave travels more than I do. He called me the next day and said that he and his wife were working in the yard after we had dinner and saw some of their neighbors walking the dog. These neighbors stopped to visit with them for a bit. Keep in mind that these are my old neighbors too, as B and I lived in that neighborhood just after we married. The neighbors asked about me, as they knew I was living with Dave and his wife for a while. Dave told them we had just had dinner and that I was doing fine and had moved into a condo nearby and told them about Hazel. They asked what happened in the marriage. Dave explained that B had multiple affairs on me and that I had hired a P.I.

ADVICE SECTION

to confirm it. They wanted to know if it was a dentist that B worked for, and Dave told them it was some guy that she had probably met in a club, and then he said The Losers name. The wife's eyes opened wide, and she told him that she knew one of his ex-wives. She used to play tennis with her. She said that The Loser had an affair with his secretary years ago, and the wife was very upset and broken up about it. I'm not sure if this was his first wife, second wife, or third wife, but she said they divorced soon after his affair. I was concerned that it could be a coincidence with the name, but I looked in the white pages of the phone book, and there is no one else in the entire area with that last name. It is not a common name, so I assume it must be him.

Dave said he couldn't wait to call me about this conversation and it is probably just a matter of time before he and B start doing the same thing to each other. Poor character and crappy values usually don't just automatically go away. They are truly a match made in heaven.

When I was searching for The Loser's name on the Internet, to see if there was anyone else in town with his name, I found out more and more about the guy. It looks like he has been involved in several lawsuits, and he and one of his wives owned a home that was foreclosed on them in 2010. I just hope he can keep his shit together long enough to keep paying the mortgage for B until such time as they can get the house out of my name or until time runs out and I appoint the receiver to sell it. So far so good; they are now making the payments on time, and I do check every month.

I just closed on my condo and could not be happier. My house payment is one-tenth of what that big house was, and I am ready to start socking money away. I recently bumped up my 401(k) contribution so that I can max it out. In addition, I am putting all of my moonlighting earnings into a tax-deferred account. I may actually be able to rebuild the money I lost in the divorce and paid to the attorneys. Of course I am a loser, according to B, for living in a condo. She has told me numerous times that I am a loser for living in a condo. I guess all the millions of people who live in condos are losers. I could not be prouder of my condo and happier about my lower house payment. If I lost my job tomorrow, I could make the house payment by waiting tables at Applebee's. It is a nice feeling to know that I am no longer strapped to a huge mortgage, insurance, taxes, and utilities.

Everything is about status and appearance to her. She has never saved a dime in her life, but she loves to show off the big house and act like a superstar. We will see what happens in January when she has to

ADVICE SECTION

get my name off the mortgage. I don't think she has a prayer of qualifying, and she certainly won't get help from The Loser, having had a recent bankruptcy and foreclosure. Maybe she will trade him in for another one soon, and this time she will do a credit check first.

I asked Hazel her feelings about the condo and if we were to get married. She said she would be happy to live in that condo forever, and that it will allow us to save more money and travel more. WOW, what a 180-degree turn from B!

Our divorce decree clearly reads that I get the kids every Thursday after school and the first, third, and fifth weekends. I certainly try to plan my travel schedule so I can get my sons as much as possible. The girls are older and are into their friends and other activities, so I don't get to see them as much.

I called my son on Wednesday night and told him I would be picking him up after school, and he said, "OK, Dad, see you then." At about noon on Thursday, I got an e-mail from B stating that she would be picking him up, as he would have to shower, and then they were going to my oldest daughter's birthday dinner. I had already told her that Hazel and I wanted to take my eldest out to dinner at the place of her choice; however, she never responded. I send B an e-mail back explaining that it was my day to get my son and that if she wanted to trade days, she should have let me know sooner. I told her that I was planning to pick him up after school, and I had better not have any trouble from her or I would immediately notify my attorney and file a motion. She e-mailed back calling me a loser and telling me that he wanted to go to his sister's dinner, and I should not try to control everyone. She said that the kids really don't like coming to visit me and went on and on with her bashing.

I politely stated that all of her opinions do not matter to me and that I would be picking up my son and I needed confirmation back from her that there would not be any issues. I even e-mailed The Loser to see if he could talk some sense into her and explain to her how the divorce decree works. Since he has been through divorce three times, he might actually understand that I want to see my son the one day this week that I was allowed to.

He e-mailed back telling me that he was in Nassau trying to catch a flight back and that he would talk to her. I am actually starting to like him more, as I believe he has tried to smooth things over with her. Anyway, I did end up picking my son up from school. We worked out and then I dropped him off at home later, as I had to fly out of town the next day.

ADVICE SECTION

I stopped by to visit my old next-door neighbors after dropping him off, and they told me about the weekend. I had my son over the previous weekend and we went to a professional baseball game, but the girls did not come around. The next-door neighbor's son (twenty-five years old) was home with a buddy on Saturday night, and they had the outside patio radio on, possibly on the loud side. He said the police came over and just walked right in the back door and said that B had reported a wild party going on. The police recognized that it was just him and a buddy playing pool and hanging out and basically apologized for the false information. The neighbors' son went next door to confront B and ask her why in the world she would call the police on him, rather than going over or calling, if the radio was too loud. She told him that she knew he once told J. Golf (me) that she came home at 3:00 in the morning, while I was out of town, and that she was trying to get him back. He did not think it was amusing.

She then proceeded to tell him that she is not the evil person in this divorce and that J. Golf (me) had beaten her and pushed her down the stairs for years. WOW! He knew it was not true but just figured she was drunk again. She also told him that his mom was a bitch. I would consider his mom one of the nicest, most Christian women you will ever meet.

◀ I WAS TRAPPED IN A MISERABLE MARRIAGE AND SCREWED BY THE TERRIBLE SYSTEM!

I visited with my former neighbors for a while, and they said they have never been so miserable in their life with a neighbor. All of their lives they have loved their neighbors, and having B nearby was the most awkward living arrangement ever. It is just a matter of time before they get the heck out of there. I feel so sorry for them.

This incident was the second time she had called the police on the neighbors. The prior time she complained his floodlights were shining in her bedroom window and she thought he might be a stalker. Later I found out that those officers ticketed all the cars that were facing the wrong direction. These were all adults who had come into town so they could carpool to the neighbor's son's wedding. How sad is that, for them to all receive $90.00 tickets from Barney Fife. This story sounds just like Mayberry.

I wrote the police chief a letter to let him know how sick it was that his officers were taking marching orders from crazy B. They would have never just stumbled onto those cars to write tickets. She told them to write those tickets, in order to mess with the neighbors, and the police officers actually did it. B has lots of cop friends in our city, and she drops their names often to get out of speeding tickets. She is so powerful!

ADVICE SECTION

I returned from a business trip on Tuesday night and was excited about picking up my son on Thursday for the entire weekend. I had no plans and figured we would just hang out, try some new places to eat, and maybe attend the Byron Nelson PGA Golf Tournament that was in town. I sent B an e-mail on Wednesday explaining that I would be picking my son up and keeping him all of my time this weekend and also needed to know if he had any activities, once again.

This time I did not get a response for almost eight hours. Suddenly an e-mail popped up and stated that my son would not be available this weekend. Oh, no. Not this again.

Once again I explained that this was my weekend, and it was not her decision whether he would spend time with me or not. She sent back another e-mail and called me a few names and then told me that it was his awesome sister's graduation from law school and his awesome grandparents were in town and that he was going to spend time with them, and he would not be available to see me. I sent a note back stating that I would be there at 3:30 to pick him up from school, and I had better not have any trouble. I never heard anything, and he never came out of the school. I could not call my son, as she has the phone blocked, so I called the school to see if he was still in there doing a project or staying late. They said he had not been to school in three days. I found out from my older daughter that they all took off to San Antonio and just plain ditched me. This incident really pissed me off, and I immediately called a family law attorney near my house. I figured I needed an attorney to help file for contempt of court. The gentleman I met with said this was indeed a violation and that my judge would most certainly come down on her and probably make her pay my attorney fees and give me some make-up time with my son. He said it would be better if we could have one more recorded incident like this, so I agreed to wait and see how it went over the next few weekends.

The judge will really be angry if it becomes a pattern. If she tries to tell the judge that my son did not want to come see me and that he wanted to go to San Antonio instead, he would respond by reminding her that a thirteen-year-old is not going to make the decisions on how to execute a divorce decree. The attorney said that B might actually get thrown in jail for a few days, if she really cops an attitude.

Well, a few months have gone by since I have written, and she has not pulled any more "hide the kids" stunts, so I have not had to haul her into court. I can't really afford the attorney fees right now anyway. I think B is starting to go crazy, crazier than she already was. She seems panicked for money. I received an e-mail from her demanding $16,500 for my oldest daughter's college expenses, when she had just graduated from high school. B did not send out a graduation announcement to anyone on my side of the family, including me. My mom, my sister, and I all mailed my daughter a check anyway. I also found out that B and my daughter had a big party at the house and I was not invited to that either. I have the three college savings accounts for the kids and thank God that I am allowed to manage them. All the funds in those accounts were contributed by me and by my father. B never added a dime to them. Now she suddenly wants $16,500 out of the account for COMMUNITY COLLEGE! I told her NO WAY, that I would not give her anything out of that account, and that I will only reimburse her for what college and books cost if she can produce receipts from the college. First off, they never consulted me about any of the decisions that were being made. She did not get accepted to any of the universities that she applied to, so she was stuck going to community college. There's nothing wrong with that; however, there is a community college right down the street from us, and we would be paying "IN-COUNTY" tuition. They picked one that is three hours away and double the price, because it is in a different county. In addition, she will have to pay room and board that would otherwise be avoided if she stayed at home. Come to find out she wants to live in an apartment with one of her girlfriends, which is considerably more costly than a dorm and a meal plan available by living on campus. I looked up the cost range on the school website and told B I would pay only for school, books, fees, and the equivalent of what dorm housing would cost.

You would think that I was more evil than SON OF SAM. B told me that I had no choice in the matter and that I had better get her a check by Friday, "OR ELSE." She also told me to read page thirty of our divorce decree, where it talks about the kids' college accounts and that they would be managed by me and would be used for the sole purpose of college for the kids. In addition, it states that it would be based on the University of Texas standard costs. I don't have a problem paying for my daughter's college with these funds, but why would I empty out half of the entire value of the account on one semester at community college? She could never tell me how she was coming up with $16,500, but I knew it had to be a scam.

My daughter recently totaled her new Camaro. Remember the Camaro? It was the car that B bought her right before she filed for divorce, a brand-new $30,000 rear-wheel-drive racecar for a sixteen-year-old, now totaled. She rammed into the back of someone, probably while texting. B and my daughter recently tried to hit me up for some money to help with the difference between the car insurance reimbursement and the cost of the next new car my daughter wanted. I

ADVICE SECTION

told them "NO, I cannot help at all, because I have no cash myself." When my daughter sent me an e-mail begging me for help, I had to explain that all my money had gone to the attorneys, since her mom dragged the damn divorce out so long. In addition, I pay $2,250 per month in child support, which is more than enough to buy some beater car to take to college.

Well, they did not like that. B sent me another e-mail and said she was taking her to register her for college and needs that money right away. I politely explained, AGAIN, that I was not going to give her any of the money out of that educational IRA and that I would only reimburse her for valid receipts and that if she was not able to front the money for her until such time that I pay her back, I would be glad to take her to school and get her registered. I have not heard from them about it since. It would not surprise me if she tries to haul me into court to complain that I am not living up to the college-expense part of our decree. I would be happy to visit with the judge about it and show the e-mail chain that went back and forth. I think B and my daughter want to use some of the college money for a car and also for furniture for my daughter's college apartment. SORRY, those things are not what the college fund is for.

B also told me that our daughter needs a new laptop computer. I bought her a brand-new Dell two years ago, so I asked what happened to that one. She said that they need a laptop that does not get viruses! HA HA! I said they can all get viruses, just go get the one fixed that she has or let her use her high school graduation money to buy a new one. She did not work one day this summer after graduating from high school. I love my daughter to death, but she has been enabled to be lazy and live a Rolls Royce lifestyle. It may sound like child abuse, but my father did not buy me any extra perks once I turned sixteen. He gave me my first car, which was an eight-year-old hand-me-down company car, and I had to pay for ALL of my gas and insurance. He always provided a nice house and my meals, but any of the extra crap that I wanted came out of my yard mowing and waiting-tables salary. It makes you appreciate things more if you buy them yourself, and it teaches a strong work ethic. My oldest daughter would just stay up late partying with friends and then sleep until about noon and then lie in the sun during the day. She does not need to go away to school. She needs to land herself a job and attend community college down the street. I just found out that she has THREE tattoos, at least. I made it very clear to her that if she chose to get tattoos, she can figure out how to put herself through college. She must have had them installed the day she turned eighteen.

The bad thing about it is that I have no control of anything anymore. The damn divorce decree states that I

ADVICE SECTION

will use that savings for her college, even though she went against my wishes. In addition, I don't have a co-parent ex-spouse that gives a damn about tattoos and piercings. She probably got a few tattoos herself, to look good on her Harley that she bought behind my back before filing for divorce. I am not prejudiced against people who have tattoos, but I just do not want my kids getting them at eighteen years old, since their frontal lobe has not fully developed, and they would probably regret them someday. I really hate the one that is on the top of her hand, as it cannot be concealed unless she wears gloves to an interview. We don't hire people at the stadium unless their tattoos can be covered. They really are not acceptable in the business world. Getting tattoos was a very poor decision by her, against my wishes, but I still love her anyway. I can't wait until the day that she comes to me and says, "Dang, Dad, you were right, I really wish I had not gotten these tattoos. " It may be thirty years from now and they may be stretched out and unrecognizable by that time anyway. I just want her to eat crow someday and maybe admit that I was right.

My son and I just went to Iowa so that my old long-term buddy Chris could give his deposition on the Bubba case. His testimony could be very valuable to my trial, as it proves she knew about the tape recordings more than four years ago. The statute of limitations is four years, and he remembers talking to her nine years ago when she complained to him that I was recording her phone conversations.

I cannot believe this lawsuit is still going forward. She has nothing to lose by going through the motions, since she found an ambulance-chasing attorney to take it on, surely on contingency. Meanwhile, I just keep paying monthly attorney bills to defend myself. My attorney did find some new case law that shows where a similar case was lost by a kid that sued a parent for recording the family phone lines, because the parent can consent for the minor child to record the child's phone calls when it is in the best interest of the child. My attorney was initially concerned, because I was not the biological father and I had never adopted Bubba; however, he found more information on the fact that since I brought her into my home and gave her a place to live and meals and clothing that I was acting as *loco parentis*, which means I had all the authority to help protect her from harm. Actually I could be sued if I had not acted as a parent to protect her. Things are starting to move in my direction, but I am not going to get too excited about anything. This case will actually be a jury trial, and you just never know what a jury will do. Even if I win, I still lose. I am into this case for about $15,000 in attorney fees, and it will probably be at least that much more for a trial. I guess it still beats the $100,000 that Bubba and her mom are trying to extort from me. It looks like the trial is set for August 26. Today is July 15.

I leave July 29 for two weeks in Africa. My mom is taking me on a very nice vacation, because she feels sorry for me about all of the money I have spent in the divorce and now this Bubba lawsuit. We will be going to Tanzania. One week is a mission trip, where we will be helping build a school, and one week is a safari. My mom took this trip five years ago and said it was the best experience of her life. It is winter time in that part of Africa, so the days should have high temps in the seventies. I have already had my many immunizations. I am really excited about going, even though I will really miss Hazel and my kids. I asked Hazel if she wanted to go with us, but she had absolutely no interest. She has problems flying to Minnesota to visit her family, so the twenty-two-hour flight to Africa is not at all appealing to her.

Hazel and I have been dating more than nine months now, and it has never been better. I respect her more and more each day and she does me. She cannot believe how strange B is and claims she is so blessed that B decided to move on to someone else and make me available. I have never felt so valued or important to someone ever in my life. I am not even sure if B is still with The Loser, as I don't hear his name much anymore. I hope he is still around, or else she may have a hard time making the house payment, and the mortgage does not have to be out of my name until January 24th. The kids said he is weird. He just sits around in the bedroom and does not talk much. Maybe he is finally discovering how much of a WACK JOB his girlfriend is. He may be getting ready to bolt on her.

I am now writing from Africa. My mom took me on a two-week trip to Tanzania. One week has been a mission trip, where we helped to paint and build a perimeter wall on an existing elementary school in Usa River near Kilimanjaro. What a beautiful place, and the temperature is great! This is August, which is Tanzania's wintertime. It is about 103 degrees in Texas right now and only about seventy-five degrees in this part of Africa. I am amazed at how poor the people are in this area, yet they are happy and friendly. No one has a car, TV, carpeting, washing machine, or dryer, and most don't even have running water and electricity. All the things we take for granted are nowhere to be found; however, these fine people are very content with life and maybe just don't even know any different. The little kids were happy to see us every day when we worked on the school. My mom and her girlfriends taught the children "The Hokey Pokey," "Do Your Ears Hang Low," and many other songs that we grew up with. They seemed happy to learn these and wanted to sing them every day.

ADVICE SECTION

While I was slaving away to help build a rock and concrete wall, it occurred to me that I am facing a trial when I get back to Texas. Can you believe that I am here helping the poor people in Africa while Bubba and her mom are trying to extort more than $100,000 out of me? I am also sick about thinking of all the attorney fees that were wasted, money that could have gone to help the poor. I gave my favorite waitress a $10.00 bill after we left our hotel, and you would think she had hit the lottery. By the way, the average worker here earns only about $5.00 per day. These are very hard-working people.

Bubba and B prefer to make their money through lawsuits and attorneys. They are looking for the GET RICH QUICK scheme. I have four more days left on this Africa trip, and it has been great, a true once-in-a-lifetime opportunity. My mom decided to take me on this trip because she felt sorry for me after the divorce. There is certainly no way that I could have paid for it. The airfare to Tanzania alone costs more than most vacations that I have taken. If you ever have an opportunity to take a safari, I would sure recommend Tanzania in the summertime, which is its winter. The weather is just like Southern California. We toured the Taragarin National Park and the Norengotar Crater. Tanzania is also the home of the Serengeti, but we did not make it there. We saw all the great wildlife you would expect to see on this trip, including elephants,

I WAS TRAPPED IN A MISERABLE MARRIAGE AND SCREWED BY THE TERRIBLE SYSTEM!

lions, baboons, cheetahs, zebras, wildebeest, wart hogs, hippos, giraffes , dik-diks (yes, that is what they are called; they are like a small deer), water buck, hyenas, ostriches, and many more.

I am back from Africa, and there sure has been a lot going on in the past few days. At one time, I was concerned that there would be no way to come up with enough substance for my book. Now I am worried that I may have to cut something out to keep it from looking like a 1,000-page medical journal.

I had the kids over the weekend when I returned from Africa. They were happy about the souvenirs I brought them, including the chocolate that I picked up at the Amsterdam airport. My middle daughter was really upset with her mom and told me that she truly believed that there was something wrong with her and that she is a psycho. Without jumping on the bandwagon of agreement too much, I told her to tell me what has been going on. The Loser took them all on a vacation to California and kept bragging to them about how rich he was and that this trip cost him $12,000. She told me that he was always trying to get mom drunk, and they spent a fair amount of time at the hotel bar while the kids fended for themselves. In addition, she could hear The Loser and her mom having sex in the adjoining hotel room, and it made her sick to her stomach. When she complained about it to her mother, they moved

ADVICE SECTION

their room into a different tower at the same hotel for the balance of the stay. They also kept telling her that her dad (ME) should be buying her a car, since she thought I was so great. She has always been very fond of me and does not allow her mom to bash me and will not buy into her lies. I have said all along that I will buy her a car myself if she lives with me, but as long as I was paying her mom $2,000 per month in child support, buying the children's cars would be her job. She could take one-tenth of that child support payment and come up with a pretty decent car for our daughter. I told my daughter that I would still live up to that statement, and if she thought things were bad enough at home, I would love to take her in. It would not have worked before, since I travel so much, but now that Hazel is here and my daughter will be driving, we can make this work. I assured her that she would have a better and more normal, peaceful life with me. She said she had already decided that she wanted to do it, as long as I wanted to have her. She cannot handle her mom anymore and Is actually afraid of her. B always makes her cry, and I have never made her cry. Her mom drinks all the time and is clearly into her new boyfriend, The Loser, more than anything else. Perhaps she will view it as good news that one of her kids wants to get out of her hair.

Well, today B found out that our daughter was planning to move in with me, and the shit hit the fan. She started screaming at her and took her phone away and took her health club membership away and told her she cannot take her clothes out of the house and even told her she would not be going to her high school. She was already registered to start school there in one week, but B said she would withdraw her. She was bullying her, just like she does everyone.

My daughter called me crying about all of this, and I said not to worry. I sent an e-mail to the school principal to let him know what was going on. This school district is VERY strict about enforcing the rule that only city residents attend. Each year, you have to bring proof of residency to register your child for the school year. I told him that my name was still on the mortgage for the home in that city and that she should not be withdrawn from school, no matter what lie B may possibly come up with. I even told him that if she sells the house, I would be happy to purchase property in that area once again when it comes time to register her for next year. She has gone to these schools since kindergarten, and now B is trying to flex her muscles and be vindictive rather than do what is best for her daughter.

My daughter always told me that she never felt loved by her mom and was clearly not the favorite. I told her that I feel like I ranked lower than the back door mat on B's priority list of favorite things, even when we were married.

ADVICE SECTION

B is going to learn that she cannot win this battle. She cannot force her daughter to live with her. In Texas, the child can make the decision as young as twelve years old, and our daughter has turned sixteen. I am planning to send B an e-mail tonight letting her know we can make this change as civilly as possible or we can do it through the judge. I honestly believe she is more concerned about losing some child support income more than anything else. If B does not agree to change the divorce decree in regards to custody, I will have my attorney set a hearing so we can get in front of the judge. I am sure B will do all she can to make this move difficult.

By the way, Hazel signed our daughter up on her cell phone plan and purchased a new phone for her. I renewed her membership at the health club, and we took her shopping to buy her all the things that B would not turn over.

Well, this is several weeks later, and I have some very good news to report, and I can finally complete my book. With B in my life, of course, there may need to be a BOOK II. She never did respond to my offer on our daughter, so we did indeed set up a court date for a trial. I am also going for custody of my son, so he can have a normal life. He may not claim that he wants to move in with me, as he knows there will be more structure, rules, and church and less video-game time. What thirteen-year-old boy would want that? I don't want him in that house where the oldest daughter is smoking marijuana and having parties at the house while the children are unsupervised. There are strange people sleeping over and sex is taking place.

I had dinner with my oldest a few months back, and she tried to justify to me why pot is not bad. She kept telling me how it has become legal in some states. I told her she would NOT win this argument and that it leads to other things, and I don't want her to be a pothead. She is angry at me right now, as I have been pressing B to get her drug tested, and B ignores me. Once again, B is acting like a friend to her rather than a parent. Someday my daughter will understand that I am just trying to be a good parent rather than the enemy. When that frontal lobe develops, I hope it will all be clear that good parents should do all they can to steer their kids away from drugs and tattoos. We will see how this turns out.

The other VERY good news is that I won my lawsuit against Bubba. It actually went to trial, because I was not willing to settle with her. She was suing me for $90,000 plus attorney fees, which were up to $45,000 prior to the trial. It was a two-day trial in county court with a real judge and six jurors. Both sides gave their testimony, and I won on every single issue. NOTHING for Bubba on her claim, and now she is stuck with a

ADVICE SECTION

huge attorney bill, as it was not structured on a contingency. Right before the jurors came in with the verdict, the senior attorney from her law firm leaned over to my attorney and said, "We will settle for $35,000 right now," and my attorney said, "No thanks!" I love it. Ten seconds later, the court read the verdict, and I was set free. I did not do jumping jacks or give a fist pump. Rather, I teared up and was thankful to God and the six jurors who exercised common sense.

Bubba and her attorneys slowly walked out of the courthouse like scolded dogs. Bubba wore a miniskirt both days and proudly displayed her tattoos. My attorney could not believe her attorneys allowed her to dress like that.

B never showed up once, even though I feel very certain she was behind a lot of the efforts to extort more money out of me. She would have loved the part where I talked about her being a serial cheater, WITH PROOF. I can go on Oprah and play those tapes at this point, and there is nothing B can do about it.

Even though I am very pleased with the outcome and did go to a very fine steakhouse to celebrate that night, a part of me is very sad. It is very sad that my stepdaughter would sue me when all I was doing was in the best interest of her and my other three kids. She may have the same ability as her mom to believe her own lies and convince herself that I was an extreme out-of-control Nazi parent. I guess the judge and jury did not feel the same. If Bubba came up to me and apologized, I would forgive her. I actually feel sorry for her, as she is a product of her mother. I am doing all I can to keep my three other kids from going down the same path.

I am going to close out now and hope you found this book to be enjoyable reading. It is all TRUE, and if you feel sorry for me, THANKS! My life is getting better every day. To think I would still be with B if she had not filed for divorce! I believed in staying in a marriage for better or worse and wanted to be there for my kids. Thank God that she pulled the trigger and not me. I never knew how good life could be without having to share a house with that troubled person. I wish her peace and rehabilitation. I have been dating Hazel for just over a year now, and we are engaged. I gave her a ring, my grandmother's diamond, at a party in North Carolina that my mom threw for us. She was surprised and shocked but actually said yes. We will probably marry on Hazel's family farm next summer and then have a nice reception party back in Dallas at the Cowboy's Stadium.

Thanks so much for reading my book, and if I ever make any money by selling it, my commitment is to reimburse myself for the amount of attorney fees I spent and then donate anything else to charity.

CPSIA information can be obtained at www.ICGtesting.com
Printed in the USA
LVOW06s0441140114

369237LV00001B/1/P